# POWER SERVE

**One Man's Experience
In Servanthood**

# POWER SERVE

**One Man's Experience
In Servanthood**

*JACK MOORE
with
Marlene Spalding*

*Acts Publishing*
... Committed to the ongoing documentation
of God's supernatural activity among men.
A Division
of
Destiny Image Publishers
P.O. Box 351
Shippensburg, PA 17257"

ISBN 0-914903-96-9

For Worldwide Distribution
Printed in the U.S.A.

# Contents

| Chapter | | Page |
|---|---|---|

# Dedication

This book is dedicated to those in all denominations who love and serve Jesus Christ with a whole heart, in any corner of the world, and are on the cutting edge of the harvest in these final days...

# Foreword

It is well known that the man with an argument is no match for the man with an experience. Even the business world prefers a man with positive experience over the man with a degree who has no experience. Experience is not only a good teacher, but it also gives permanent instruction. It is difficult to forget what you have learned by living.

John, the apostle, began his first epistle by saying, "That which was from the beginning, which we have heard, which we have seen with our eyes, which we have looked upon, and our hands have handled, of the Word of Life ... that which we have seen and heard declare we unto you" (1 John 1:1,3). He could find no higher authority to attest to what he was about to write than his own personal experience.

Jack Moore has done similarly. In sharing with us the many and varied experiences of his walk with God, he speaks with the authority of one who has been there. This is not a book of theory or even theology; it is a book of encounters that have affected the lives of many.

I found myself yearning to participate in some of these victories with the author. I put the book down with a greater awareness that the Holy Spirit did not cease working through men and women at the close of the life of Paul.

The book is interesting, challenging, and refreshing. It is a "must read" for today's Christian.

Judson Cornwall

# Chapter One

# The Kiss of a Servant

*"And whosoever will be chief among you, let him be your servant"* (Matt. 20:27).

The oppressive, putrid air hung heavily like thick, dusty drapes. Mosquitoes hummed continuously everywhere, and I frequently slapped at my face and arms. Light green lizards darted over the stucco walls in hopes of lunching on a few of the crawling flies. Beyond the confines of the small building, street vendors shouted to hot, milling throngs. Their cries mingled with the raucous calls of ravens and the shrill blastings of horns from various vehicles.

Two whirring ceiling fans helped little to disperse the mix of odors from one hundred fifty bodies seated shoulder-to-shoulder on the scrubbed cement floor.

My eyes scanned the white-garbed pastors and Christian workers assembled for this special convocation to ordain ten men. Some had walked barefooted up to thirty miles in the hundred-plus temperatures. Others would have had a tortuous train, bus, lorry or bicycle ride.

Soon it was my turn to speak. God had directed my attention to the subject of love, as He had the two pastors who had spoken before me. But each message was different.

The Spirit led me to thread my way back through the crowd of men, and as I did so they moved aside to allow me room.

"You must love as Jesus did. He that is chief among you, let him be your servant," I continued. "Serve one another in love."

I stood before one particular young man seated halfway back in the room. "Inasmuch as ye have done it unto the least of these, my brethren, ye have done it unto Me," I called out, gazing into the deep brown eyes of an Indian national.

Then I heard God's voice instructing me to do something unthinkable in India, or almost anywhere. "Kiss his feet," He directed.

I paused, thinking of the startled reactions my obedience could produce, but knowing I must obey. Kneeling, I noted the leathery brown skin, calloused from years of exposure to dirt-filled, hot streets. But as my lips met the top of one dusty foot, God's power, like a jolt of electricity, burst through the room. Men, crying out under the Spirit's anointing, embraced one another. Many knelt to do as I'd done. For two hours they expressed their love for one another while bewildered wives peered from outside through the open doors and windows. Repentance, forgiveness, mercy and love flowed freely. In a country where time matters little, it meant even less on that sticky Sunday afternoon. I'd never be the same; nor would they.

I later learned about the overseers' plans to remove from ministry that day the young man whose feet I'd kissed. But the God of forgiveness and restoration had other plans. The wayward Christian worker would become a faithful, loving pastor.

I'd learned many years before that obedience to servanthood is the key to God's power; and the imminence of Jesus' return requires that I always obey immediately. Although no man knows the day or hour of His coming, to live in daily obedience ensures one's readiness to meet Him.

To confirm the reality of Jesus' soon return, God gave me a vision in 1979. While kneeling in prayer one evening, suddenly a large hourglass appeared. Red sand trickled through its narrow neck. But as I watched, the neck widened until sand rushed through to the lower glass. Then God spoke. "I am bringing this age to a close rapidly," He informed me. A year later He repeated the vision and words.

We must be about the Father's business. To delay is disobedience.

So I serve now, not only desiring to please the One who so transformed my life, but to fulfill the purpose to which I'm called before Jesus comes.

The preparation for my spiritual insight began much earlier than this, however. In fact, I knew the reality of God early in life. It started with my grandmother on a farm in New York.

# Chapter Two

# Christ Appears

*"...Suffer the little children to come unto me, and forbid them not: for of such is the kingdom of God"* (Mark 10:14).

There had been no rain for two months, and the hot dust lay heavy in the road. It seemed a perfect place for a seven-year-old boy to run barefoot, and I glanced back gleefully to see dust bursting into clouds behind me as I ran toward the farmhouse.

"This is great!" I thought. But Grandma and Grandpa didn't think so. This one hundred acre farm near Falconer in Western New York was their food source. With the corn dying and potato leaves already brown, food would be scarce for winter.

My grandparents, Swedish immigrants, were hard workers — up at five each morning and working side by side all day. Grandma plowed, planted potatoes, pruned the orchard, milked the cows, and still found time to cook up delicious Swedish dishes, such as korv (a kind of sausage) and pickled herring.

This day, with warm brown dirt still clinging to my toes, I bounded into her kitchen.

I'd recently come to live with Grandma and Grandpa.

My mother, in ill health, had given me to my aunt and uncle. Aunt showed me a real mother's love. How I enjoyed her bedtime stories and chats as she rubbed my back! But their problems (Uncle was an alcoholic) prompted Aunt to turn me over to Grandma and Grandpa, who had had twelve children of their own, many of whom had died early in life.

I had a special love for Grandma. She was a short, stocky, jovial lady in her long, plain gray dress, whose deep facial wrinkles often erupted into smiles.

But today was different. Concern clouded her face. She reached her hand out to grasp mine as she spoke her favorite name for me: "Barn Lilla" (Little Boy), "Let us go and pray. I believe now that it is time God brought the rain."

Hands joined, we entered the living room and knelt on the creaky linoleum floor.

Grandma prayed simple, expectant prayers, and today's went something like this: "Father, You know that our crops are dying, and You know that that's our food. We would pray now in the Name of Jesus that You would send Your rain and let us have a good harvest. Amen."

Suddenly the most wonderful thing happened. By the time we could stand and look out to the south, the sky, which moments before had been cloudless and brilliant with sunshine, was blackening. Dark clouds were skimming the horizon. Within minutes, a beautiful rain pelted the windows, soaking the ground and saving our crops.

Grandma's simple prayers and simple faith impressed me. They were my introduction to God, to His Son, the Lord Jesus Christ, and to the power of His Holy Spirit.

We seldom attended church, since it meant a six-mile horse and buggy ride to a service my Swedish-speaking grandmother found difficult to understand.

Nevertheless, Grandma was close to God and I knew He was real in her life.

Although I was told years later that Grandma couldn't read, I'd see her reading her Swedish Bible by the kerosene lamp each evening, even after a long day in the field. And she read to me. I loved to hear about the crucifixion of Jesus. The tears would course down Grandma's cheeks and I'd feel so warm inside. She radiated His love, and because of her life-style I hungered for Him.

How I loved to go out behind the house at night and gaze at the stars! I'd fall to my knees as if some power had captured me. I didn't understand anything theologically; but I knew, at eight years of age, that there was a God in Heaven. Jesus was real, and when I prayed I could feel spiritual arms around me. I would weep for joy, not knowing why.

Each night I curled up on my bed, a daybed beside the living room's potbellied stove, under the warmth of Grandma's handmade quilts.

I hadn't been asleep there long one night when I found myself behind the house, standing beside the old Bartlett pear tree.

Suddenly I was conscious of a brilliant white light. I squinted and looked for the source. As I turned my head upward toward the southeast, there was Jesus in a white robe, arms outstretched. Although the light hid His features, I knew His face was filled with love.

Then slowly He descended until finally He was standing beside me. Bending down, He gently swooped me up into His arms and together we began to ascend.

Here I was, a young boy on a farm. I had a dog, ponds to splash in, woods to hide in, streams to wade in, frogs to shoot, dandelion greens to pick and cook, dusty roads to run down, trees to climb. I was happy with all the things and freedom any boy could want.

But I'd never before felt such joy. I began weeping, sobbing so hard that I awoke. As I sat up, realizing the importance of the dream I'd had, I exclaimed, "Oh Jesus, why couldn't You have taken me? Why couldn't You have taken me?"

I learned that nothing in the world compares with an encounter with Jesus Christ.

# Chapter Three

# The Fire

*"But above all things, my brethren, swear not, neither by heaven, neither by earth, neither by any other oath..."* (James 5:12)

I stirred from comfortable sleep under the puffs of quilts and blankets, and out of the corner of one eye caught sight of dancing ribbons of orange on the wall opposite my bed. As realization dawned, I flew to the window like a stone flung from a slingshot.

"Grandpa, the barn's on fire!" I yelled.

Grandpa was already scurrying into clothes, having awakened about the same time as I.

The nearest neighbor lived a half-mile away; but suddenly neighbors appeared from everywhere out of the night. The old faithful pump behind the house kept belching buckets of water as the helpers formed a brigade to put out the fire.

But aside from saving the chicken coop, their efforts brought little reward. The fire had gotten quite a head start, lightning having found a target for its devastation.

Just as the first threads of light wove their way across the blue-black of dawn, Grandpa and I silently stared at the heap of smoking beams, the remains of what represented Grandpa's life's work. Tears ran unchecked down my sooty cheeks. I turned my eyes to study Grandpa's face and viewed despair etched in the tired lines.

We were poor before this. Now with his hay, wagons, buggies and tools gone, Grandpa would have to start all over again. He wasn't a quitter, but at his age it would take a long time to regain what he'd lost.

I knew Grandma would do everything she could to help. She had always made her own butter and sold some to the Witkop & Holmes grocery truck. Colorful hand-hooked rugs graced the plank floors throughout the house; but others she'd designed had been traded for staple goods. Yes, Grandma would not only provide words of encouragement, but she would also produce whatever she could to help Grandpa make a living for us.

A few days after the fire, Grandpa called for his constant companion, Rover, a loving collie that herded the cattle at the shrill command of a brass police whistle. Rover, in obedience, ran for his master on a straight course through the still-glowing coals which lay under the black remains of the barn. The dog's sharp cries because of his horribly burned paws hurt Grandpa even worse than the loss of his barn. As he knelt over his dear friend, it was Grandpa's turn to weep, and he did. Rover, the favorite of all his animals, had to be killed.

So excellent had been the dog's corralling of the cows that they continued to herd themselves at the sound of the whistle, as if still under Rover's expert direction.

Much later I learned that Grandpa and Grandma had had an argument, a rare occurrence, just days before the fire. Somehow the barn had figured in their disagreement. Angrily, Grandpa spoke words foreign to his usual imperturbable nature.

"Then damn the barn!" he'd shouted.

And damned it was.

# Chapter Four

# She's Gone

*"Precious in the sight of the Lord is the death of his saints"* (Ps. 116:15).

What fun it was to bounce down the country roads with my cousin Bob in his '31 Chevy! At sixteen I appreciated this degree of freedom Grandma allowed me.

This autumn evening we were enjoying one of our jaunts when the car stopped abruptly. Bob and I weren't too surprised at the interruption, since carburetors were prone to collect dirt. Usually, though, the problem could be solved with a screwdriver and pair of pliers.

Dusk afforded little light, so Bob lit a match to study the situation under the hood. The match burned evenly and brightly until suddenly, with no breeze, no reason, as if a hand covered it the flame went out.

"Grandma just died," I exclaimed, not understanding my burst of knowledge or realizing it was a Word from the Lord.

Bob closed the hood (we made no repairs), hopped in the car, and it started with no problem.

The few miles back to the farmhouse seemed long as

I pondered the beauty of Grandma's life and wondered what I'd do without her.

Grandpa had died two years before and Grandma and I had run the farm together. Our life was good, but I chided myself for not being more helpful and obedient. However, I'd continued to learn about Jesus from Grandma's faith and life-style.

"Your grandmother just died," an aunt said tearfully as I entered the old farmhouse, confirming what I'd already known.

Grandma had been sick, but it hadn't seemed serious, so we'd given her illness little thought.

Relatives and a couple of neighbors had already gathered in her bedroom. I pressed through them to look at this precious lady with the smiling wrinkles, the smiling mouth, the smiling eyes. Joy filled her face. In that moment I knew that death, for those who believe, is a good time.

I ran the farm alone for several months while attending high school six miles away. It was a rigorous schedule: up before five, build a fire in the kitchen woodstove, then hurry off to the barn. Quickly I'd break the ice in the creek and lead the cows to water. Then it was time to put down the hay, bring the cows back in for milking and prepare their fodder for the day. Chores done, I gobbled a breakfast, jumped on my bicycle and headed for school. Drifts that winter often forced me to carry my bike for several miles. Once or twice I was grateful to get to the neighbors' in time to hitch a ride to school.

After I hurried home, at 4:30 p.m., my routine began again: build a fire in the stove, do barn chores, eat supper, study, and drop into bed at ten.

My only fellowship was with the cows and cats who occupied the barn together. They became my special friends and I'd rub their heads and talk to them as if they understood the deep hurt and aching within me. With no electricity, no radio, and the nearest neighbor a half-mile away, my kinship with the animals filled some of the silence.

Of special comfort during the hours alone were the faith instilled in me by Grandma and my prayer times in this old farmhouse with the many memories lingering around me.

Cousin Bob and his wife came to visit one day. Somehow an argument ensued.

"My mother says..." I began.

"She's not your mother," Bob interrupted. "She's your aunt."

"Of course she's my mother. I have her name," I countered.

"No, Ingeborg is your mother," Bob yelled, referring to the woman I'd known all my life as "Aunt Inky."

I stared in disbelief while his words reeled in my head. A sickishness crept over me as the trauma of his revelation grabbed at my stomach. No one had shared the truth until that moment. I'd thought my true parents were the aunt and alcoholic uncle who'd first raised me.

I left the house so I could cry alone, feeling broken under the burden of words that had pierced my whole identity. I thought of my aunt, the woman who had shown me such love and tenderness in my early years. Then I thought of my mother, and waves of rejection washed over me. In all my life I'd not known a worse moment. Later I'd learn the rest of the truth — that I was the illegitimate son of a teenage girl.

The rigorous schedule soon took its toll, and after a few months I became ill; but my illness provided the opportunity for me to know my mother. Having regained her health, she took me into her home and nursed me with much love and good food. Part of Mother's therapy as a Christian was large doses of God's love.

Mother saw me graduate from high school in 1943,

and two weeks later kissed me good-bye as I left for the army.

But always, as I thought of home, my mind would slip back to the old farm and Grandma's warm kitchen, and I'd hear her voice saying, "Barn Lilla, let us go and pray."

# Chapter Five

# A Brush with Death

*"Bless the Lord, O my soul, and forget not all his benefits ... Who redeemeth thy life from destruction..."* (Ps. 103:2,4)

Terror gripped the fifteen men in the CG-4A glider as it shook violently over the marshalling area in France near Germany's border. Death seemed imminent in this flimsy aircraft, fashioned only of light alloy tubing and covered with paper and glue.

These fragile crafts had proved, however, to be a quiet way to deploy troops behind enemy lines at night during World War II. Along with the ease and silence, though, was a high casualty rate, the gliders often colliding with church steeples, treetops or even enemy tents. Sometimes they were targets for incendiary bullets. Then the simple structures were consumed in six seconds.

We were volunteers attached to the 326th Glider Paratroop Infantry, and in order to qualify for the additional pay it offered, three flights per month were required.

The tow plane pulling us through the air was a two-engine C-47. Three gliders in formation were attached by heavy-duty nylon lines. Today's was to be another routine flight with the gliders floating silently back to the airport where we'd started.

The time for release came; but instead, the nylon line still pulled us at nearly one hundred fifty miles an hour.

"Your tow line didn't detach," I yelled to the pilot as the flexible rope stretched taut and the tremendous shaking began. Fear overwhelmed the men, and some, in panic, prepared to jump minus parachutes.

A miscalculation — the glider pilot had tilted too soon, not pulling the release first — caused the rope to wrap itself around one wing. The plane's pilot, suddenly seeing the problem, slowed to allow slack, but I envisioned the wing ripping off at any moment, plummeting us to a certain death.

Quickly I prayed, then watched as the rope mysteriously unwound and slipped free. The sudden release catapulted us with a jerk, but we were okay. I could only imagine that an invisible hand had released us from the noose from which we'd hung in mid-air.

Having glided beyond our target by now, we began searching for a suitable landing spot.

"Don't stretch your glide!" I yelled to the pilot. "There's a wheat field below."

Early in my training I'd learned the danger of trying to get too much distance from one glide. The result would be a stall and nose dive.

Safely landed, we jumped from the craft. Never had ground looked so good. Our shouts of joy obliterated the shouts of the farmer, angry because of the swath we'd carved in his wheat. Several of the men even kissed the ground. Some refused further glider flight, their brush with death having sufficiently quelled the thrill of dangerous adventure.

But I flew on, unafraid, knowing God was with me. My rude introduction to the military had begun at

Camp MacKall in Fort McClellan, Alabama, the draft choosing me two weeks after high school graduation.

I was being trained in survival tactics as well as infiltration and demolition techniques in the Infantry Pioneer (Engineer) Corps. Later, I'd learn how to kill a man with my hands and feet in several different ways in eight seconds.

The outfit was assured that by the end of training we'd be able to survive anywhere. Many of us wondered, however, if we'd survive the training. Some men didn't. "Short rounds" (ammunition with an insufficiency of powder, causing it to fall too soon) killed two or three men as they crawled along the infiltration course. Then there was the "old man" who, at age thirty-five, lost his mind, and the boy who cried every night, missing home. Another slashed his wrists in a suicide attempt.

Temperatures often exceeded one hundred degrees as we marched fifteen to twenty-five miles, lugging sixty-some pounds of equipment and supplies in our field packs.

Often we were overwhelmed by thirst, but had been cautioned over and over of the danger in drinking during these long, hot hikes. Ignoring the warnings, the fellow ahead one day kept guzzling water from his canteen. Suddenly he collapsed in front of me and later died.

Not many, however, had serious problems with following orders. We soon learned that the discipline was for our good, and that if we could obey, our chances of survival were excellent. Later I'd learn how true this is in the spiritual realm as well.

Rounds of live machine-gun ammunition burst three feet over our heads as we crawled along the fifty-yard infiltration course planted with explosives. Coiled barbed wire had to be cut and crawled through. Blistered hands and wrists were the rewards of our success. We quickly understood how this place had earned its name: "hell-hole."

The rocky terrain and cliffs added to the training ground and we learned to step silently through the darkness and rain. Danger threatened with every inch of our treks in the dense black nights. Each man would break a firefly and stick it on the back of the man ahead to make following easier.

Soon after arriving at Camp MacKall, I'd seen a notice posted in regimental headquarters for an Army Air Force O.C.S. (Officer Candidate School) test one could sign up to take. Welcoming a challenge, I added my name to the list.

Just prior to D-Day, while I was on maneuvers, a jeep zipped up and halted nearby. The captain jumped out and approached me.

"You're in the Air Force," he announced.

"But I don't want to leave," I protested. Initially I'd wanted to join the Air Force, but my step-father had urged me toward the Army. Now my thoughts were of the men I'd come to know. We'd anticipated being shipped out and serving together.

Back at regimental headquarters I learned I'd scored very well on the O.C.S. test. I also learned that in a week or two I'd have had sergeant's rating. I was pleased with my accomplishments, but sad to be leaving my unit.

Within hours I was on my way from Alabama to Florida, headed for initial basic training via Pullman coach. Soon I'd be sent to Catawba College in North Carolina for further studies and training.

I was overwhelmed with the reminder of God's hand on my life when one day the news reached me that none of the men in my company at Fort MacKall were heard from again after D-Day. God had indeed intervened, and I felt a heavy responsibility to make my life count for Him in some way. Sorrow for the men I'd loved poured over me, but I thanked God for saving my life.

# Chapter Six

# Into the Unknown

*"Thou shalt not be afraid for the terror by night; nor for the arrow that flieth by day"* (Ps. 91:5).

We left the States for LaHarve, France in a grossly overloaded liberty ship, the command ship of a convoy. For as far as we could see to the left or right were ships. This one was crammed with three thousand men, the whole 13th Airborne division.

Our path zigzagged across the ocean for thirteen days. Then we anchored for a few hours at Hampton Harbor, England before continuing across the English Channel to our destination.

I had boarded with everyone else in the New York harbor. Three decks down I'd found my bunk, a canvas cot. Tiers of such cots, with narrow walkways between, filled the 30 x 40 foot room. My bed was just inches above the floor. To squeeze my six-foot frame into the small space between my bunk and the one above seemed like an overwhelming task.

"Lord, I'm going to die or go crazy," I quietly cried out. "I'll never survive this." But immediately I went off to sleep. The claustrophobia I'd first felt never returned.

Nearly all the men were seasick during the rough voyage. I wasn't, however, and believed God was keeping me from illness.

On our fourth day out we learned that ships in the vicinity were being torpedoed by German subs. Suddenly, in the room filled with noisy bodies in cramped cots, we bristled at what sounded like a chain dragging across the bottom of our vessel. The room quickly quieted. A few voiced their concern, wondering if we'd hit a mine. Simultaneously, something hard bumped my behind. Feeling under my bunk, I touched the bolt of someone's M-1 rifle. It had slid across the floor. Immediately I knew the source of the strange noise. I'd wanted quiet in the room and smiled in the dark as, without divulging my knowledge, I got what I'd wanted. The room remained still and soon everyone was asleep.

Most of our time was spent in the chow line, since there were so many men to be fed. We'd finish one meal, and an hour later it was time to get in line for the next. Often, when a soldier forgot to hang on to his metal tray, it slid down the slippery metal table with the listing of the ship, wiping out several other trays in its path.

Far below the deck the top of the black water shimmered in the streams of moonlight as my three buddies and I hung over the railing. Only the diesel engines and swish of water rushing past the bow broke the silence. Soon one would voice his thoughts, which matched ours. Will we return alive or in a coffin? Will we be blown to pieces, our remains scattered somewhere in the dirt of a foreign country?

I wanted to serve, but wasn't interested in becoming a hero with my name carved on a monument back home. I didn't want to have to expend great courage. I had a job to do. I was anxious to do it and return. I suspected that most men held similar feelings. Even then, however, the assurance of God's Presence brought a quiet to my mind.

Upon entering LaHarve harbor we faced the horrid realities of war. Remains of sunken French ships protruded from the murky water. We'd arrived in the middle of the night. Yet people skittered down dark streets, darting into alleys or the basements of bombed-out buildings. There were neither street lights nor lamps in windows. There *were* no windows. The dark seemed to swallow us as we marched toward camp.

Suddenly a bright light pierced the blackness like an omen of promise. It was merely a bulb suspended on a wire over a Red Cross donut and coffee wagon; but it was a beacon for some tired, lonely soldiers. The kind gesture, coupled with smiles and friendly conversation, was dwarfed, perhaps, by the long shadows of war. An old wagon, a bare light bulb, some refreshment — unforgettable symbols of caring hearts. They reminded me that in one small act, we can be a beautiful light for someone in need.

Knee-deep mud from the spring thaw filled the mine-strewn field. We watched our every step, uncertain whether all the mines were marked.

Our three-hundred pound sergeant, while running through the field, hit a jeep mine with one heel and set it off; but it misfired. However, it renewed caution. We were quickly introduced to the dangers of war.

Excitement and tension filled the camp before each mission. We were to be dropped behind enemy lines. Before midnight we went over and over the checklist, sharpening and resharpening gleaming bayonets. The "Black Widow" surveillance plane would often discover waiting Germans at the intended target. Once, just half an hour before takeoff, the plane returned with infra-red pictures showing our landing site surrounded by 88-millimeter guns. Had we landed, we would have been wiped out.

There was always sufficient opportunity for men to deny their moral standards. For a candy bar or cigarettes a girl was happy to go with a soldier. Women approached guards on duty, offering themselves to the lonely men. Many resisted the advances; a few didn't. Only by God's grace and strength did I avoid the temptation all around me throughout the war. I was thankful for His help, for I knew I couldn't have resisted alone.

Once while traveling through France, our train had an hour's layover. A friend and I decided to wander into the nearby village. Passing through it, we hiked on into the green countryside. There we came upon a Gypsy camp.

"Cigarettes, cigarettes," called a man from behind a wood-rail fence. Beside him stood a beautiful, smiling, black-haired girl, his wife or sister, we figured. He motioned to her and to the house. We'd heard of men succumbing in such situations and being knifed. Our uneasiness forced us back toward town and the train.

As lifeguards, my friend Jerry Russell and I had access to a rowboat which we often used. One sunny afternoon as we rowed, I caught sight of a young woman and called to her in French. From the bank she answered in perfect English. We rowed over to find a mother and her fourteen-year-old daughter, Monique. I became acquainted with the family and from subsequent visits in their home, learned of the hardship war had imposed on the country's people. Monique's family was without heat or food. They didn't even have shoes. Piles of blankets helped to keep them warm.

Monique, whom I affectionately nicknamed "Mosquito," became like a little sister to me.

The day came when we were to be shipped out. The whole 326th regiment filled the public square. As we sat on the grass awaiting orders, a girl threaded her way through all the men. It was "Mosquito," coming to kiss me good-bye. Most of the men hadn't known of my relationship with the family, so heckled me about "holding out on them." They assumed that Monique, who looked much older than her fourteen years, had been my girlfriend. I merely smiled, enjoying the attention of a pretty little French girl.

We became part of the 82nd Airborne. Our outfit never took a prisoner. We killed them. The elite German SS did the same. Many in my outfit were wiped out. Later I'd be awarded two battle stars, but I never had to kill a man, an answer to my prayers.

Once I was ordered to guard a prisoner given us by the ground infantry, only to find that our captive was a fragile little boy, not over fourteen or fifteen years old. His too-big German uniform hung loosely on his small frame. I wanted to cry. While walking him to the tent I grieved that children weren't exempt from the hideousness of war.

On V-J Day, when the war was over, someone fired a shot in excitement. It whizzed through my tent, inches from my head. How ironic it would be, I thought, to be killed after the war had ended, and by a comrade's bullet, at that. Again I thanked God for saving my life.

Soon we boarded a victory ship, again overloaded, for the voyage home. Remembering the cramped quarters of our ship on the way over, I chose a berth in one of the gun turrets and wrapped up in sleeping gear. Although I was subject to the elements, it was better than a narrow cot below.

With an intense storm, huge waves washed across the rolling decks as we approached New York harbor. I hung on tightly to the gun turret railing. The welcoming lights of New York intermittently disappeared as we pitched in the rough water. But they seemed to convey a message. "It's time to resume your dreams," I imagined them saying to us.

But then I thought of the thousands of men who would never again see what I was seeing as the ship rose to the top of another towering wave. A horrible sense of the loss of men I'd known, killed on D-Day, and thoughts of their families' sorrow welled within as my emotions matched the water's turbulence. Soon, though, my sad thoughts were replaced with the joy of feeling home ground under my feet, seeing the crowds, and hearing the bands and happy shouting. I'd returned. How I thanked God.

# Chapter Seven

# Cancer and Arthritis
# - Crucibles of Hope

*"And we know that all things work together for good to them that love God, to them who are the called according to His purpose"* (Rom. 8:28).

"Doctor, I'm a Christian," I stated simply. "God is with me. Please tell me what's wrong."

His eyes studied me from under wrinkled brows.

"You have a serious arthritic condition," he intoned with thoughtful concern. "Your spine will fuse, and sometime later you'll have unbearable pain."

As the doctor recited his findings, I could feel the renewing power of the Holy Spirit coursing through my body; and though my mind told me I should be upset, there was joy and peace instead.

The place was Youngstown, Ohio; the year, 1955. Because of a job promotion, I'd been transferred here from Jamestown, New York. I was thirty, had a young wife, June, two sons, and had anticipated a bright future.

We'd joined and become active in the Disciples of Christ Church in Youngstown. I was an elder, June and I worked with the youth, and we were involved in a small home group called "Yokefellows."

But even with all my involvement in the Yokefellows and with the church, I'd become painfully aware of two things: I no longer had either the strong sense of the Lord's Presence dwelling in me or the warmth I'd known when praying out behind the farmhouse. In fact, it seemed that God wasn't listening.

Also, I'd realized that, despite all my church activities, I didn't know how to serve the Lord. There was no fruit from my efforts. I was troubled.

One day, taking a sheet of yellow ledger paper, I drew two columns. At the top of one I wrote, "What I have done for God," and in the next, "What God has done for me." It was a startling revelation! In the first list, I scribbled: elder in the church, served on various committees, presiding over some, taught Sunday School. But when I began listing what God had done for me, I ran out of room. It was a stark moment of truth. Frustrated, I began searching my mind for Scriptures pointing out what God says about serving Him.

As I studied the writings of St. Augustine I'd found that as his relationship with Jesus Christ deepened, he realized the Lord considered some of his doings to be great sins. Augustine knew he had to deal with them. His first prayer went something like this: "Lord, deliver me from this evil, but take Your time." Not until later, as his knowledge and understanding of the Lord developed, was he able to submit his whole life —to kneel and give it totally to God.

I judged that my prayers had carried a similar thread of reserve: "Okay, Lord, there are certain things in my life I want to hold on to. I'm not ready to give them over to You." But now I wanted to serve God the very best way I could. I was ready to say, "Lord, I give it all to You." I knew that without His help and revelation I couldn't even understand His Word.

It was then that I dropped to my knees. "Dear Lord," I cried out, "Somewhere along the line I've lost the wonderful feeling of Your Holy Presence. You filled me when I was young, and I could feel You moving in me every time I knelt to pray. Lord, I seek the renewing and regeneration of Your Holy Spirit. When I call upon Your Name, I want to feel Your holiness, Your Presence.

"Father," I continued, "I must confess that, as much as I've studied Your Word, and in spite of the Bible courses I've taken, I really don't know how to serve You. I'm asking You to open my eyes so I can see; open my ears so I can hear how to serve You. O God, I ask forgiveness for my weakness. Help me. In Jesus' Name. Amen."

A quiet assurance crept through me and I knew God had heard my prayer.

Now, a week later, I sat peacefully in the orthopedic surgeon's diagnostic room, listening to his report. Pain in my back and in the sciatic nerve of my left leg had forced me here. Pointing to the x-rays, he noted the problem areas.

"I don't know of any medicine we can give you to cure this," he added. "I don't even know of any pain pills or injections you could take to relieve the pain as this progresses."

The x-rays showed that the left leg was considerably shorter than the right, aggravating the arthritis and causing great pain when I walked. He said I'd need an extra heel and sole added to my left shoe.

"Doctor," I said, "I have a growth that I'd like you to examine, too."

He took a quick look.

"That's not in my field," he explained. "But I'll call a friend of mine who's a specialist."

In two days I was seated in another doctor's office, and on the third day found myself in the hospital. The tumor was cancerous, although of a slow-growing type.

However, the doctor added that it could move up my spine, touching all the vital organs.

God had prepared me well for this moment, as I recalled the beautiful sense of His Presence I'd had that first day in the doctor's office. Now I knew the reality of God's Word — that His perfect love casts out all fear (I John 4:18).

In the following days, June, facing the possibility of my death, came to the hospital for *me* to cheer *her*. She would leave renewed and restored after I shared the joy and peace God had given me.

We read in God's Word that ALL things work together for good to those who love the Lord and are called according to His purpose (Rom. 8:28). I had to accept the fact that it included cancer and arthritis.

One morning, feeling quite good, I slipped out of my hospital bed, donned shoes (the left one built up by now) and robe, and ventured out into the hall. Prompted by the Holy Spirit, I entered the room across from mine and greeted the two gentlemen occupying the beds. After chatting briefly, I turned to leave.

"By the way, what's wrong with you?" one of them asked. "Oh, I have cancer," I replied nonchalantly, and continued on my way back to my room.

"Hey! Hey, wait a minute," he called. "Come back in here. I want to talk to you." I reentered the room to hear his next question.

"How can you be so happy if you have cancer?" he queried.

Without hesitating, I extended my hand, palm up, and explained, "Well, first of all, I'm in God's hand and in His care. He has the very hairs on my head numbered. He's given me an opportunity to prepare my life to meet Him." I added that my sorrow was not for me, but for one who doesn't know Jesus Christ, who perhaps steps into the street and is killed. I finished with that and left.

As I rounded the corner of my bed, it happened; a

voice, God's voice, spoke clearly and with great authority. To me it was audible: "For inasmuch as ye have done it unto one of the least of these, my brethren, ye have done it unto Me."

I stood transfixed, overwhelmed that He'd given me a revelation and understanding of His Word in response to the question I'd asked so desperately some days before. As many times as I'd read this Scripture, I'd not fully understood it. Now I had new insight: if I wanted to serve Him, then I must serve my fellowman. He was saying that He's represented in everyone. It's He who is within that addicted, fallen man in the alley who hides a bottle in a tattered brown bag. It's He who is within the company president. It's He whom we are helping when we assist our neighbor wherever we find him. Then He added, "Even when your wife has a need, if you fill that need in her, you're doing it unto Me."

"Oh, my!" I thought. "How many times I've missed the opportunity to serve You, Jesus, in this way, both with my wife and others."

I took two steps and again He spoke.

"Let your light so shine before men that they may see your good works and glorify God in heaven."

Again the revelation was swift in coming — when we do anything that edifies and lifts up the Lord, then His Name is glorified, His Name is magnified. It isn't always the "big" things we do. Even the smallest acts bring Him glory.

I heard Him again.

"Your testimony glorified Me in the presence of those two men."

The truth seemed so simple — that as we give ourselves over to Him, His light shines through us. As we help others, He's also in them, and we are serving Christ.

I saw with new clarity that we can't separate our love for God from our love for man. Jesus was quick to say that as we love our Father with our total being, we must go on to love our neighbor as ourselves.

First John 4:20 says, "If a man say, I love God, and hateth his brother, he is a liar: for he that loveth not his brother whom he hath seen, how can he love God whom he hath not seen?"

# Chapter Eight

# Eagle's Wings

*"But they that wait upon the Lord shall renew their strength; they shall mount up with wings as eagles; they shall run, and not be weary; and they shall walk, and not faint"* (Is. 40:31).

"It's a miracle!" the doctor exclaimed following one of my weekly examinations. He'd not anticipated my tremendous recovery.

After my surgery, a team of five specialists had been assigned to my case. None were certain that all the cancer cells had been removed. At our first meeting they had recommended x-ray therapy — forty-eight treatments, 600,000 volts each for sixteen minutes a day.

"Do whatever you feel necessary," I'd said, still basking in the sense of God's joy and peace.

I'd need assistance in making the daily trip to the hospital, they insisted, since I'd be too weak to drive. I'd also need pills for nausea, a side effect of the treatments. For that, a simple pregnancy tablet would be prescribed. A further result of the treatments would be the shortening of my life span by eleven years, the doctors calculated.

As if this weren't enough, they frankly stated I'd be unable to father normal children. They'd be deformed.

The doctors admitted they didn't know the outcome. But before I'd left the hospital, I'd purposed in my heart that, whatever the results, God would have His way and I'd believe Him to give me strength beyond the physical strength I'd need.

How good it seemed to be home again with June and our two boys, Dennis and Jim!

On the following Monday the daily hospital visits began. But despite what the doctors had predicted, I was able to drive myself.

Blue tracings on my back, pinpointing the areas where the radiation would be applied in a lead-lined room, added to the strangeness of my situation. Sixteen treatments, I was informed, equalled major surgery. So by medical calculations, I'd suffer the shock of four operations, each in a different part of my body.

However, I discovered treatment time to be perfect for meditation, and God's peace prevailed. My prayer became, "Lord, You know I don't want to die. But whatever Your perfect will is for my life, let it be so."

Without knowing that eleven a.m. was my therapy time, people were led to pray for me at that hour each morning. They were friends, Protestant and Catholic; what comfort I gained, knowing that God even had His hand on the time of prayer! I felt His love cutting across all denominational boundaries upon learning that Catholic friends had had a mass said for me.

Weakness ensued after several treatments to my stomach area. But God prevented the predicted nausea. I had a natural resistance to taking the pregnancy pills and was happy I didn't need them.

I soon learned that God wanted me to use my time in the hospital for His purposes. His Spirit impressed upon me that there were people I was to visit. So each day, upon leaving the x-ray room at 11:16 a.m., I trudged to the chapel and spent several minutes in prayer, asking for God's guidance before making my way from room to room as He led.

I loved this little room. It was like an oasis in the desert, providing me with the spiritual refreshment I needed both before and after times of visitation. The warmth of the padded oak pews and tiny altar made this a very special place to meet with the Lord.

Although God instructed me not to preach, many times He allowed me to speak about Jesus. Most often, however, I was simply to hold patients' hands, assuring them that someone cared for and loved them.

I gradually noticed that as long as I was calling on the sick and sharing God's Word, I felt no weakness at all, nor was I hungry. Curiously, though, I also noticed that the few times I went to my office I was immediately overcome with fatigue and forced to go home to bed. With that, Isaiah 40:31 came alive; I saw that in waiting on the Lord my strength was renewed.

Each time I met one of the specialists he'd shake his head, amazed at my recovery. Although I'd not see the completion of my healing right away, it was evident that divine power was at work — I needed no pills for pain or nausea, no transport to the hospital. And I was spending two to three hours visiting hospital patients, at times assisting the chaplain or nurses in comforting someone. I was beginning to walk by faith instead of being bound by circumstances.

"Yes, this is a miracle," the doctor reiterated.

I'd not forgotten the doctors' verdict that the x-ray therapy would cause a chemical change in my body, producing a deformed child should June and I have another. But it didn't change my desire. I'd dreamed of having a quiet, demure little girl snuggle up in my lap. The dream stuck in my heart, remaining unchanged along with the doctor's word when I consulted him again. I knew it was time to confer with the Great Physician.

"God, I want a daughter," I prayed. "I'll do my part; You keep her healthy."

Nine months later I stood in the maternity ward hallway of the Youngstown Hospital, gazing through the window at our eight-pound-plus daughter, Mary Louise. She was perfectly healthy, and the tears poured down my face in gratitude for God's mercy.

"You surely are happy about this child, aren't you?" commented a passing nurse.

"Yes," I replied emphatically, and began telling her of the kind of cancer I'd battled, plus the x-ray therapy.

"No wonder you're so glad!" she exclaimed, staring at me in amazement.

How sad that we so often limit God when He can do all things. But how wonderful it is when we take God at His Word so He can bring those wonderful, victorious moments into our lives.

He didn't stop blessing us there. A year and a half later He added another beautiful, healthy daughter, Nancy Jean.

# Chapter Nine

# Learning His Ways

*"I can do all things through Christ which strength-eneth me"* (Phil. 4:13).

Screams pierced the quiet of the hospital hallway. I envisioned someone near death with doctors and nurses hovering at the bedside, and chose to tiptoe on past.

"Mr. Moore, Mr. Moore!" the chaplain's secretary called, running to catch me. "Do you know how to give last rites?" she asked nervously.

"No, I know nothing about it," I answered.

"Well, there's a lady dying," she said, "And the family wants last rites for her. The priest and chaplain aren't available. I don't know what to do."

"I can pray," I uttered spontaneously.

"Oh, good. Come with me," was her immediate reply, as she quickly led the way toward the origin of the screams.

My knees weakened as we approached. "Oh God, what have I done this time?" I silently questioned. "They're expecting a man with a priestly collar to come in and do whatever they do; and here I come, only able to utter a prayer. Oh God, make me a vessel. Use me. I don't know what to do. Speak through me."

We entered the semi-private room as I finished my hasty prayer. Passing the first bed, we approached a drawn curtain around the second. The secretary pulled it slightly open and pointed to an emaciated young woman, then left. I stood staring at sunken eyes and cheeks in a contorted, jaundiced face. Light brown hair lay limp and tangled on the wet pillow. Foam bubbled from her mouth. Later I learned she'd been incoherent for three days. She writhed, screaming and groaning by turns. Another woman, her sister, sat numbly beside her.

My feet seemed riveted for an eternity to one square of gray tile. I wanted to run, but a force propelled me until I stood directly over the dying woman. The same force moved my arms until my hands clasped hers —yellow hands that in the natural I'd recoil from touching; but in the touching she became silent.

Quite suddenly the silence was broken by a soothing voice speaking some of the most beautiful words I'd ever heard. Perhaps it was half a minute I listened before realizing the words were falling from my own lips. The prayer continued for two or three minutes before I heard, "Amen." At that the woman's eyes fluttered open and a sweet smile stole over her face.

"Thanks, Lord; thanks, Lord; thanks, Lord," she softly spoke.

The dramatic change was startling and I was overwhelmed at the unusual way God had used me. The sister suddenly jumped from her chair, grabbed her purse, and digging out her money, thrust bills into my hand.

"It was God," I told her and explained that I couldn't accept pay. She insisted, however, and I was happy to accept fifteen dollars for the chaplain's office.

As my unsteady feet led me toward the door, the lady in the first bed stopped me. "Young man," she said, "I'm Catholic and I have never heard a more beautiful prayer in my life."

"Neither have I," I said. "It was God."

Two weeks later, during another visiting time, a voice called to me. I turned and recognized the sister I'd met.

"Oh Reverend, you're the man who touched her life. Would you come in and pray with her?" she asked.

As we approached the bed, the young woman opened her eyes and smiled. I took her hand and began to pray quietly. Joy radiated from her face and I sensed she was seeing something heavenly. The beaming smile reminded me of the one I'd seen on Grandma's face at her death.

In the next moment, the woman closed her eyes and was gone.

I'd learned something more about God's greatness and faithfulness. I'd learned, too, that God will equip us to do whatever He requires of us. I wasn't to judge my weakness, but rather count on His power.

The sister had called me "Reverend" only because of the prayer I'd prayed initially. It reminded me that all Christians have an awesome responsibility to do the work of the ministry. Titles are unimportant. Only obedience counts with God.

*******

After x-ray therapy one day, I spent an unusually long time visiting the sick — the young, the old, the dying, the lonely, the confused. The longer I visited, the heavier my heart grew.

"Jack, if you had faith the size of a grain of mustard seed, you could say, 'Be healed in the Name of Jesus.'" The statement echoed in my mind.

I'd never prayed for someone to be healed before, nor had I witnessed a divine healing. It wasn't that I didn't believe the Lord could heal. I not only believed He could, but that He would. If He'd created the body, I figured He certainly could recreate it. But how, I asked myself, could I pray in faith for the sick and see them healed? As I drove home the question haunted me.

"Oh, God," I prayed, "There must be an answer to this. You've shown me how to serve You. Now I don't know how to pray for Your sick and have faith to believe for their healing."

Arriving home, I dropped on my knees in the bedroom.

"God, I read Your Word, but don't fully understand," I prayed aloud. "Father, I want to see the sick healed as they were when Jesus walked the earth," I continued. "You've said if Your Word abides in me and I abide in You, I can ask what I will and it'll be done. Father, is my faith so weak?" I implored. "Is it my weakness that's prohibiting Your healing power from flowing? Father, forgive me if what I'm praying is wrong. But I ask for a revelation — a revelation that would open Your Word on healing to me. Father, I believe it's important to have a whole ministry. So reveal what I need to know. In Jesus' Name, Amen."

Emotionally spent, I eased myself onto the bed and carefully lay on one side, unable to lie on my back because of the surgery.

Suddenly, a peace seemed to envelop me. I could identify with the apostle Paul who, writing of the trance he experienced, didn't know whether he was in or out of the body. I was rolled gently onto my back with no pain.

Next, a hand appeared before my eyes. Simultaneously, I heard a voice as I lay suspended in that spiritual realm. The words spoken appeared on the hand: "I am God and, remember, you are human. All you must do is trust, trust, trust, trust, trust."

Proverbs 3:5, "Trust in the Lord with all thine heart: and lean not unto thine own understanding," was alive.

As the hand faded, as the voice quieted, as the

resounding of "trust" ceased, I was rolled back onto my side. I lay quietly, waiting for the revelation I knew God would give. Soon it came.

"Don't you know that I, the Lord God Almighty, know every heart? Didn't I put all the stars in the heavens and call them each by name?" I heard in my spirit. "I know the hearts of everyone in the hospital. I know the hearts of those who are well. And all you must do is trust in Me. You must become My vessel and speak what I give you to speak by My Holy Spirit, since I know the hearts of all people and what's right for them. So you are to be a vessel through which My Holy Spirit can speak."

A week or so later, as I ambled down the tiled hospital corridor, the Lord spoke again.

"Go into the dormitory room at the end of the hall."

I'd avoided the busier dormitories, preferring quiet conversations in private and semi-private rooms. But the direction was unmistakably clear and I turned my steps in obedience.

I was surprised to find five empty beds. The sixth held an elderly lady, and at the foot of the bed stood a nurse I knew. She quietly checked the patient's chart.

"This lady's eighty-two years old," she informed me in a low voice as I approached the bed. "She has cancer from the top of her head all the way down through her body. We're trying to make her comfortable. She could die in the next few days or in the next hour." With those words she left.

I moved to the side of the bed and stared at the frail ninety-pound figure. Tubes extended from her nose and mouth while a sense of death clutched the corners of the room.

A voice spoke: "Ask her if she knows she can be healed in the Name of Jesus Christ." The command caught me off guard.

"Why, Lord? Why would you have me do that?" I

inquired. "She's so far gone she can't even hear me."
But I remembered my promise to obey.

Bending over the railing, I whispered into her ear.
"Do you know you can be healed in the Name of
Jesus?" I moved my ear to her mouth and waited.

"Yes," was the whispered reply.

Amazement that she'd even heard my question
registered in my mind and I reflected on the meaning
of her "yes." The impression that she'd merely offered
the expected answer crept into my thinking and I
tiptoed from the room and its air of death.

The following day the same urge to visit her pushed
at my steps and again I complied. Again, also, God's
voice commanded me. "Ask her if she knows she can be
healed in the Name of Jesus."

How strange, I thought, that I'm being asked to do
this a second time. But in obedience I whispered the
same question. "Do you know you can be healed in the
Name of Jesus?"

"Yes," came the weak reply.

"She's only saying what she thinks she ought to say,"
the Spirit said. So I left.

When on the third day I was commanded to do as I'd
done the first two days, I was puzzled at the leading of
the Lord. I was even more puzzled at the repetition of
this question-and-answer period after three more days.

On the seventh day, with the same leading, I
cautiously entered the room and heard the same
command as before. "Ask her if she knows she can be
healed in the Name of Jesus Christ."

I dutifully whispered the question as before and put
my ear to her mouth to hear her familiar answer. But
the "yes" that erupted from her fragile lungs on this
seventh day was so forceful that my ear was filled with
her saliva. I suddenly knew that today's reply had been
forced out by the faith growing in her during the past
six days.

I dug a handkerchief out of my back pocket to dry my

ear, and then headed for the chapel to sort out my thoughts. They played a tug-of-war in my mind.

"Lord, she's eighty-two years old. And if she loves You and believes in You, wouldn't it be better that she go to be with You now?" I asked. "She wouldn't have any more pain." I paused, then conceded. "But for some reason, You want to heal her and I know Your ways are not my ways. So Father, in the Name of Jesus Christ, she will be healed."

A finality settled into my mind and I left the hospital for the day.

As I pondered this strange event, the story of Elijah was quickened to me from First Kings 18. "Go up now. Look towards the sea," he'd told his servant, who answered, "There is nothing." But Elijah was insistent. "Go again seven times." And it was on the seventh time that a little cloud appeared, indicating that rain was on its way.

Then in the fifth chapter of Second Kings we read about Captain Naaman, who was stricken with leprosy. The command to him from Elisha was to go into the dirty Jordan River and wash seven times. "After you do this, you will be clean; you will be healed." This was difficult for Naaman to understand. But when he did as he was told he was completely healed. He couldn't have been healed had he dipped in the Jordan six times. He had to obey and dip that seventh time.

In the repetition of the question to the woman filled with cancer, God was saying, "Trust Me. Do what I tell you and don't give up. Don't waver and you'll see the results. You'll see My power manifested."

Back I headed to the dormitory on my next visiting time. What a beautiful surprise awaited me! I found the woman fully clothed, sitting in a chair, waiting to be discharged. She appeared ten years younger, having gained weight and color.

On all my previous visits the nurse had been absent.

But this time she stood by the door, as if anticipating my arrival.

"What happened?" I asked.

"You wouldn't believe it," the nurse replied.

"Well, try me," I quickly answered, anxious to hear the details.

"All the cancer's gone and she's totally healed," the nurse shared. Vital signs had suddenly so improved that new x-rays seemed necessary, she added.

A couple, relatives I presumed, waited to take the healed woman home.

Kneeling by her chair, aware that she probably didn't know me, I whispered, "We know what happened, don't we?"

An immediate "yes" came from her lips.

"We'll always praise God and give Him the glory, won't we?"

Another "yes" followed, and with that I left, revelling in the knowledge that God had taught me something more about obedience. He was emphasizing the importance of doing everything His way.

Awe wrapped itself around me as I realized that if I'd stopped short of speaking the seventh time, this lady would have died. And I'd have missed seeing one of God's miracles.

"This is just for you. Don't share the story now," the Spirit of the Lord said after this, the first healing I'd ever seen. God wanted to give me more experiences to develop my understanding. Much later He'd release me. "Share it wherever you go," He finally instructed.

# Chapter Ten

# Quick to Obey

*"For we walk by faith, not by sight"* (II Cor. 5:7).

Shirley was a tall, fourteen-year-old black girl who had been burned over much of her body and was not expected to live. I met her during one of my visitation times and found she loved the Lord.

She lay strapped to a Stryker frame and I began visiting her particularly at noontime so I could feed her.

I watched Shirley move past the death stage and past the terrible itching by singing praises to the Lord. She would sing psalms until her mind was totally concentrated on Christ. Then the itching subsided.

I was there when this lovely girl walked out of the hospital, completely healed, and I knew I'd learned a beautiful lesson on the power of God's Word.

Someone told me about Mabel, a widow. Severe depression had closed around her after the death of her husband. Then four days later her brother died. He'd been her only remaining relative. Added to her losses was the amputation of one leg because of sugar diabetes. With all of these tragic events, Mabel had lost the will to live.

With my lunch, a sandwich, in my pocket, I began visiting her during the noon hour. Over our lunches we chatted and soon became friends. In the process, her attitude toward life seemed to brighten.

When Mabel finally became well enough to leave the hospital, June and I were so attached to her that it seemed only right to take her into our home. There she became a happy part of our family for a time, and we felt privileged to share in her life.

Some of my experiences I didn't understand, like the one I had with Mrs. Jacob. But I had promised God that I would simply be obedient, ministering as He directed.

Although only in her forties, Mrs. Jacob was dying of cancer. I made a habit of visiting her, spending three to five minutes each day.

Then one afternoon, as I stepped quietly into her room, I saw the face of Jesus superimposed on hers and somehow knew that this would be the last time I'd see her alive. So I spent twenty minutes holding her hand and praying with her.

After I arrived home, the expected call came from her husband — she'd gone to be with the Lord.

I'd had no leading to pray for her healing and didn't know why. But in my first experience of praying for one to be healed, God had said, "Trust, trust, trust." I knew by then that it's not for us to do anything more than what the Holy Spirit says.

Another time when I prayed for someone I saw a cemetery and knew they'd soon die.

"Don't you think I know his heart?" the Lord queried. "You speak what I have you speak."

I'd learned that the results had nothing to do with an individual's sickness. After this, I never had a problem with the situation. So I prayed, "Lord, please take away the pain," when I had no leading to pray for healing.

Elizabeth was another such case. She was afflicted at age seventeen with the same kind of cancer I had. Her father and mother were precious people, as were her brother and her boyfriend, who was planning to be a minister.

Through Elizabeth's trial I saw great joy in her life.

Finally she improved enough to return to school for a time. But later she confessed to me that she found herself weakening spiritually in the face of peer pressure. So much at school seemed to draw her allegiance away from Jesus Christ.

"This is a good experience because it keeps me close to the Lord," Elizabeth confided in me.

Her boyfriend, John, who was praying earnestly for her healing, asked me to join him in agreement. Something in my spirit held back. So my prayer was, "God, have Your way in her life."

When the cancer hit Elizabeth's spine, she became paralyzed from the waist down.

"Take her home," the doctors urged her family. She'll die within a month, anyway."

So I began making daily visits to her home. Three months went by, three months the doctors hadn't expected, while John continued to pray for her healing. But I sensed that God had another plan and that her witness would be in a different way.

Late one afternoon after my visit, Elizabeth's mother, Grace, called me into the living room. The sun streamed warmly through the window, reaching the soft chair where I sat. Grace's voice broke the silence.

"Jack, we have to release Elizabeth to God now. We know it's not God's plan for her to be healed.

"Are you sure?" I asked, wanting her to be certain of the decision.

"Yes," came the quiet but definite reply.

"Okay, God," I prayed. "We release Elizabeth to you." A strange knowing that she was loosed to meet her Lord pulsed through me.

"She's gone," Grace informed me in a phone call as soon as I arrived home.

Elizabeth had been a witness to everyone who

visited her. They'd come to her hospital room to draw from her cheer. In her sickness she was spiritually strong. But apart from her time of illness, she drifted away from spiritual things. She had no fear of dying. There was no sadness. Elizabeth was happy to go to be with the Lord.

Then there was Bob, a respected attorney in the church June and I attended. He had a lovely wife and family with whom we were friends.

One night Bob phoned to tell me their beautiful teenaged daughter had been hit by a car. Her face was badly cut. A deep gash extended from her forehead all the way down one side of her face, and she wasn't expected to live.

"How's your faith, Bob?" I asked.

"My faith is all right," was his choked reply.

"Then please don't worry. I'll be right over," and with that I was out the door.

As I entered the hospital room, God gave me a word of knowledge. "She will live," I heard in my spirit. "And there will not be a scar."

In the natural I knew that without radical plastic surgery there would certainly be an ugly scar on the girl's face. However, in a remarkably short time, not only was she healed, but just as God had said, there was no sign of an injury.

God was saying to me, "If I speak it, you can speak it, no matter how impossible it may seem."

A nurse approached me one day.

"Would you go and talk with that man?" she asked, pointing to a room near the nurses' desk. There I found a young man, about seventeen, with a broken knee. He'd been causing some disturbances and the staff thought I might help him.

After greeting him, I began chatting about sports while noticing the comic books and junk literature stacked on his bedside table.

"I've got something much better for you to read that I think you'd really appreciate," I stated firmly.

"What's that?" he quizzed.

"In the drawer there's a Bible," I said, pulling it out.

"I'm not interested in that," was his quick reply.

"You may be surprised. If you take this Bible, put your fingers right in the middle and open it," I said, demonstrating, "You'll come to the Book of Psalms. Now start reading the Psalms, nothing else."

Within one day when I again visited him, the other material was gone and he was engrossed in the Psalms. The staff had been able to put another patient in the room with him, his attitude having changed so drastically. Now he appeared bubbly and cheerful.

As I stuck my head into his room one afternoon, I noticed an elderly man in the other bed. His daughter, whom I learned was a nurse, was his visitor.

I spoke to the teenager, "Boy, it's a good day, and we can rejoice when the Lord's with us."

"Well, that's easy for you to say," the elderly man's daughter injected. "But if you had the problems we have, you wouldn't be able to say that."

"Lord, what do I do now?" I mentally prayed. "You want a witness on this, don't you?"

"Yes, I do," I heard in my spirit. So I entered the room and moved close to the young woman.

"I'm not saying this to embarrass you. You're a nurse, aren't you?"

"Yes," she answered abruptly.

"Here's the kind of cancer I have," I said, going on to share my medical problems.

"I'm in the hospital right now because I just had x-ray therapy. I've already had surgery. I've got an arthritic spine, plus a few other things."

Her face reddened.

"I'm saying this to give glory to Jesus Christ," I continued. "You can never tell how far a frog can jump by his looks, and you can't tell the problems a person has by looking at the outside. But when we have Christ in our hearts, we have joy no matter what the circumstances."

The boy was nodding in agreement.

"You'll see people groaning and moaning; but you may see somebody with a big smile who's carrying things you have no way of understanding. I don't know how long I'm going to live. You know enough about cancer, and this type can hit my spine at any time. But I have no fear. In fact, I feel great just the way I am," I concluded with a smile and retreated from the room.

God had given me the words to speak and I knew I had to leave the results with Him.

\* \* \* \* \*

The call to go see Tommy came from someone who knew of my hospital ministry.

Tommy was a nine-year-old boy whose tragic story was told in the *Youngstown Vindicator,* the local newspaper. The boy had been sledding on Mill Creek Park's "Suicide Hill," an appropriate name for the steep but popular place for winter play. Tommy's sled, out of control, had slammed into a tree, causing him severe brain damage.

The doctors' prognosis left no room for hope. He'd probably never regain consciousness, they said. And if he did, he'd be paralyzed. Already he'd been in a coma for nine days.

My visitation time usually followed morning therapy; but I was led to visit Tommy in the evening.

Quietly I stepped along the familiar corridor to the private room he occupied. A dim light glowed, outlining the motionless features. A registered nurse stood attentively at his side. I began speaking softly to her about the Lord and His wonder-working power. Tears welled in her eyes and spilled down her cheeks.

"Have I said anything to offend you?" I asked.

"Oh, no, sir," she answered. "But there was a young minister who just left, and I told him that with my experience as a nurse, I know there is no way this boy could be healed by the doctors, only by God. And he said, 'Oh no. God doesn't heal today. That was only when Jesus was here. The doctors will have to do it or he won't be healed.' "

The forcefulness of my reply startled both of us: "He may be wearing the cloth of a clergyman, but he is not a man of God. Now let's see what God will do."

We prayed together for God's healing power to come into Tommy and restore him to health.

The phone call the next day contained happy news. Tommy had made a miraculous recovery; he was completely healed. He was the same noisy, wonderful boy his parents had known before the accident.

How sad that so many people, even clergymen, claiming to know the Word of God deny His power, just as Paul cautioned Timothy (II Tim. 3:5) "...having a form of godliness, but denying the power thereof." And he advised Timothy, "From such turn away."

Jesus Christ came to save the lost and heal the sick. Then through the power of the Holy Spirit He passed that power on to others, commanding them to do the same.

As I continued ministering in the hospital, I'd first visit the chapel. There I'd pray for several minutes, asking God to direct me to the people He wanted me to see.

One day I entered the room of a slight, short Italian man. The warmth in his face reminded me a bit of my grandmother, and I began stopping every day. I was there not to preach, but to simply share the love of Christ.

After several days of visiting, I found him preparing to leave.

"Take his hand and let him know you love him," the Lord prompted. So I obeyed.

"None of my relatives like me," he informed me in his broken English. "Nobody shows me any love.

"But you know, some-a-day I'm a-gonna be walking down the sidewalk, and I'm a-gonna look across the street. I'm a-gonna see you, and I'm a-gonna say, 'There's a man that I love!' "

Tears sprang to my eyes and I swallowed hard as I gazed at this little man. It was as if I saw all humanity somehow represented in him as, in that moment, I understood a bit more about Jesus and His love.

"...Inasmuch as ye have done it unto one of the least of these my brethren, ye have done it unto Me."

For a year and a half I'd witnessed God's healing power as I ministered in the hospital. Still I wore a lift in one shoe because of the arthritis. As for the cancer, the doctors couldn't be sure it was gone.

The first time I'd tried to take a step without my special shoes, I passed out from the intense pain. Afterward, sharp pains immediately shot up my left leg and into my spine with each step minus the built-up shoe. I could wear no slippers, take no casual barefoot stroll on a sandy beach.

"God's healing all these people; why not me?" I posed the question to myself one day. He'd taught me how to serve Him, I considered. Now I could be healed.

I dropped to my knees. "God, I really believe You want to heal me," I stated. "I'm going to buy regular shoes. In the Name of Jesus Christ, back be healed. Pain, leave my body."

With that, I quickly set out for the nearest shoe store. How exciting it was as I took my first painless steps in a handsome pair of men's shoes. At home it was delightful to scuff along in old slippers.

One day much later, after seeing God heal legs, I decided to check mine. Extending my legs in front of me I found them to be of equal length. I had no idea when God had stretched out my short leg. I'd not felt the healing, but the evidence was there.

No more cancer or arthritis could be found. The miracle I'd needed was complete.

# Chapter Eleven

# Revering God's Name

*"Thou shalt not take the name of the Lord thy God in vain: for the Lord will not hold him guiltless that taketh his name in vain"* (Ex. 20:7).

I'd been taught to reverence God's Name and I always had, with one exception.

I was sixteen and tinkering with an old farm engine in front of Grandma's garage. I'd hooked the battery to it through the coil, increasing the juice to the spark plug. Foolishly, I'd taken the spark plug out, leaving the battery and coil attached to the end, with the idea of shorting out the plug. I was anxious to see if there was a spark left.

Suddenly, the battery activated the coil. The jolt of electricity jerked my whole body, stiffening my right arm straight out like a Nazi salute. In shock, I blurted out God's Name. Even greater than the electrical charge was the awful awareness of what I'd spoken. Immediately I dropped to my knees, crying out in fear and remorse. "God, forgive me," I begged.

The sensitivity I'd felt then as a teenager I still had many years later.

I'd walked into the hospital room of a church member and was troubled to hear him continually using God's Name in vain.

"Should I tell him?" I asked myself. I looked from this sunny room into the courtyard below, gazing absent-mindedly while the Lord kept saying, "Tell him he's using My Name in vain."

My heart burned to rebuke him, but I feared the man's reaction. "Lord, do you really want me to say something?" I silently questioned.

Suddenly, my attention was riveted to something strange happening outside. Tall maple trees which passed this second floor were bending over, the tops nearly touching the ground. There was no wind and the courtyard was enclosed, so I knew this was an impossibility in the natural. I stared at the pheno-menon, and although I didn't understand it, I was certain that somehow God meant it as a sign to me to get my attention. I was learning that if God wants something done, He may cause a supernatural occur-rence to motivate us to obey.

"Did you know you've used the Lord's Name in vain?" I asked the man. Immediately the trees popped straight up again. No, he'd not been aware of his words, and apologized. The ensuing conversation provided opportunity for me to counsel him to honor the Lord and not be careless in conversation.

One day a while later I was in the barbershop when a father and his young son entered. The father was swearing and using foul language continuously as he climbed into the chair next to mine.

"Lord," I prayed, "If You want me to talk to him, then make an opening in the conversation."

The minute I prayed that prayer the barber asked him, "How's your baby doing?"

"It's not good," the man said. "They thought it was a blue baby. Now they don't know. The doctors can't do anything about it and all we can do is pray."

God then spoke to me. "I've given you your opening."

I turned and looked straight at the offender. "Sir, don't expect God to answer your prayer."

"What?" he questioned, startled.

I repeated my statement. "You've been sitting there taking the Name of the Lord God Almighty in vain," I continued. "Foul language has been coming out of your mouth with every sentence. You have a child there. The Word of God says if you lead one of these little ones astray, it would be better for you to have a millstone hung around your neck and be dropped into the water. Your life is in jeopardy by the very conversation coming out of your mouth. You're sitting there and saying with that same foul mouth that you're going to go to my Father and say, 'Help my baby'? Don't expect an answer until you clean up your act and begin to revere God the Father, who is able to do all things."

The shop was quiet except for the click of scissors. The barber standing behind him nodded in agreement. I steeled myself against the punch I thought the father might deliver. But he didn't move.

Often in similar circumstances God has led me to say, "Look, that's my Savior and He's yours, too. Stop it." But always I must respond with what He tells me.

\* \* \* \* \* \* \*

The *Youngstown Vindicator* had a column called the "Hall of Fame," written by Esther Hamilton, a well-known columnist. She scouted the area to find people who had done good deeds, then wrote about them in her column.

One day I was surprised to find myself the subject of her column. She'd learned of my regular visits to one of the hospital wards — a place for some of the down-and-outers. I loved going there and conversing with the men. Sometimes I toted little gifts. It wasn't a chore, but a real joy — something I looked forward to. And it didn't seem noteworthy, especially since I was merely trying to be obedient to God's direction.

"If you humble yourself, you'll be exalted," the Lord reminded me from Luke 14:11.

A few months later I found that Esther Hamilton had again elected me to her "Hall of Fame."

About this time I was asked to speak to the youth of the city about job-seeking skills, and I was to include something about the Lord in my talk.

I did almost nothing to prepare. The Lord had put words in my mouth before, and I expected Him to do that in this situation.

The day arrived, Mill Creek Park was filled, the reporters were on hand, and the time came for me to speak. But my mind went blank. Finally, after much hesitation, I gathered some thoughts. But I wouldn't have given my performance a very high grade. I'd expected a small group and no reporters. To my embarrassment, my poor speech was written up in the newspaper.

God taught me a valuable lesson that day.

"You relied on Me when you could have done some of this yourself," He said. "You had time to prepare. I'm there and I'll do those things you can't do. But I'm not going to make a weakling out of you."

My speech could have been very good. I had knowledge in hiring. I'd even taken a course on the subject at Ohio State University. I could have spoken with confidence because of the information I'd gained.

Many times I've been asked to speak extemporaneously. Then God comes to the rescue and gives me the words.

I'd done something quietly and been awarded with an election to the "Hall of Fame." Then I'd been given an opportunity to do something openly and was brought low. I've never forgotten that important lesson God taught me.

\* \* \* \* \* \* \*

"I will never be a pastor's wife," June declared emphatically. I could understand her reluctance. She felt unqualified to enter into that type of relationship with the Lord, with me, or with other people.

It was 1957 when I first suggested to June that perhaps God was leading me into full-time ministry. In spite of her feelings, she agreed to accompany me to Maine to visit a seminary there.

After being told I would be accepted and could pastor a small church, I prayed much to find out God's will. I believed that if He wanted me to do this, He would provide for our family's needs.

With the hospital ministry, opportunities opened for me to speak in churches and to various groups. I'd been well-received when I'd spoken, and it was then my interest had deepened in sharing the Gospel of Jesus Christ with those who hadn't heard.

There was also the appeal to my intellect. In three years I'd have a Doctor of Theology degree, and I felt I could serve God better with the additional qualification.

As I'd ministered in the hospital, I'd often been mistaken for a professional clergyman, and many times found myself thinking of the discrepancy between clergy and laity. Many people have difficulty comprehending that someone not involved professionally in ministry can know and be a witness to the Word of God. They fail to realize that the Gospel went forward in the early Church from ordinary folk who simply took the call of Jesus Christ seriously, becoming witnesses in their own areas.

The position of a servant or minister isn't relegated to preachers, priests or theologians. God uses anyone who loves Him, who has a heart to serve.

"You do more in fifteen minutes in this hospital than the clergymen can do in a week," the chaplain said after one of my visits. I was humbled, but saddened also to think that the impact of the Gospel is often greater from the life of a person who simply loves the Lord and shares the message of His love without thought of remuneration.

As a so-called layman, I felt a need to apologize for witnessing, and did so to the local rabbi during one of his usual hospital visits.

"Don't ever give up the strong witness you have for the Messiah," was his sharp rebuff. "Had it not been for those witnesses, the Christian faith would not have been kept alive."

His words sank into my spirit as I realized their import. "And I, even though I'm a rabbi," he continued, "know that it's the Christian faith that's helped keep our faith in God alive."

And so my hospital visits continued six days each week. One day, after a time of prayer, I heard a clear Word from the Lord: "I want you to be My minister in business."

June was relieved that we'd be able to proclaim the Christian message through our life-style rather than from a parsonage and pulpit.

# Chapter Twelve

# A Lesson in Releasing

*"...Judge me, O Lord, according to my righteousness, and according to mine integrity that is in me"* (Ps. 7:8).

The thick fog wrapped around my car like a giant cotton spectre in a seeming attempt to isolate me from familiar surroundings. Squinting didn't help as I crept along the road leading me to the airport where I was to catch a flight for a business trip.

I'd already had one delay, having to return home for my forgotten wallet. Now I'd come about as far as before, following the clouded taillights of a car ahead, moving about ten miles an hour. Then the line of cars crawled to a stop. There we sat as if captured by a gray ghost. Later I learned that a twelve-car pileup in the other lane had blocked the road.

Suddenly lights flashed in my rearview mirror as a car hurtled out of the fog. I stiffened and in the next instant heard the deafening sound of crunching metal and glass. The impact ripped the seat loose and I was thrown forward over the steering wheel, into the windshield.

After several minutes, I staggered from the wreckage to find the driveshaft shoved into the motor and the radiator crumpled back into the car. Like dominoes pushed by a giant playful hand, I'd been crushed into the car ahead, doing hundreds of dollars worth of damage, and that car, in turn, had hit the next.

I was certain the person behind me had been killed, the front of his car having been chewed clear to the dash; but to my surprise he was walking. So grotesque, however, was his head, that he resembled a monster from a horror movie.

Besides a whiplash, I had eye and brain damage; but the insurance company was fighting payment. I had to get strong new glasses for my badly impaired vision.

As the weeks slipped by, I was having total memory lapses. In mid-sentence a thought would leave and I'd have to cease conversation.

My job was increasingly difficult, but I'd determined not to stop. Trying to stay busy, I worked outside in the yard. I didn't know then that the insurance company had posted a man in front of our house to take pictures of me, attempting to prove my lack of injury. Even pictures of the car were taken at angles which portrayed the least damage.

Friends advised me to sue for $250,000 since my eye and brain damage were already in my doctor's records. But I knew I couldn't do that. So I waited.

A year passed. Before the accident I'd needed two thousand dollars. "If I could just get the two thousand," I thought. But the insurance investigator didn't believe my claims.

Then one day a new investigator appeared at our door. I told him about the car and my physical condition. I explained how my neck tightened if I simply heard a tire squeal. I further told of my stand as a Christian.

Soon I was sent to the insurance company's doctor. My clammy palms indicated severe nerve damage. He confirmed my own doctor's findings, shaking his head in disbelief at my symptoms.

When I arrived home, two insurance company

representatives awaited me. I knew then the company's fear that I'd sue when my condition was verified. They carried a release form and a check.

"You needn't worry," I assured them. "I'm a follower of Jesus Christ and I won't sue you, even though you're a big company." But they anxiously pushed the release form into my hand.

As I looked at the check for two thousand dollars I remembered, with a smile, the amount I'd owed. Carefully I signed the form.

Over the next few days I realized that God, with His healing power, had touched me. My eyes and brain were freed from all damage. I was totally healed. Then I knew that if I'd sued and won, I'd have had a large sum of money, but I'd never have experienced the healing which awaited me in my act of obedience to the Lord.

******* 

Woodworking had been one of my favorite hobbies for many years. On this particular evening I was cutting a piece of wood on my table saw for one of the boys I taught in Sunday School.

Suddenly the wood seemed to "explode" in front of me, catching on something and spinning me around at the same time. Looking down, I saw I was missing the end of my right index finger.

Five interns studied the ragged fingertip. Their first attempt displeased them. "That's a mess. Let's start over," one suggested.

"You'll never have a fingernail," another declared. "There's a little piece of root left, but it'll only grow a sliver of a nail. It'll just be an irritation."

I permitted them to remove the remaining root, knowing God could perform a miracle.

"It's impossible," the doctor had declared as he carefully wrapped the white gauze around my finger.

"Lord, I need a nail on that finger," I quickly prayed afterward.

Not surprisingly, within two weeks a tiny new nail was already showing. Not only that, the resulting complete nail was "heavy-duty," about twice as thick. I knew it was God's abundant provision for my damaged finger. To this day, my extra-thick nail remains as a beautiful reminder of God's care.

# Chapter Thirteen

# Cleaning Up My Act

*"Let your light so shine before men, that they may see your good works, and glorify your Father which is in heaven"* (Matt. 5:16).

"How long are you going to be a sloppy Christian?" God clearly asked me one day as I took another swig of beer. I sipped cocktails during social hours before business meetings and enjoyed a beer on a hot summer day.

I knew that maintaining the profile of a committed Christian in the corporate world could often pose difficulties, since it's not fashionable to uphold Christian principles in business situations.

"That isn't necessary," June commented on occasion when I'd drink with customers. However, in my early career years it was ingrained in me by management that drinking was a part of wooing business prospects.

Although I wasn't a heavy or regular drinker, at special functions sometimes one drink led to another. Then I'd be disgusted with myself and my situation. Still, I believed I had to "fit in" in order to further my career.

Hospitality rooms were set up and the generous

amount and supply of drinks were meant to impress both prospective and regular customers. As I moved up in management and on to other companies, liquor simply was poured out in higher-priced places. Instead of taking customers to the Ritz downtown, we now courted them in Waikaiki or the Bahamas. But it was liquor and had the same effect.

When God dealt with me about the social drinking, I switched to gingerale or 7-Up in my glass. Friends became suspicious after a time and began sniffing my drink. At first their comments were negative. But slowly I gained a new respect. I also found I was having better relations with the customers. Others who were struggling with a drinking habit seemed to draw enough courage to make similar stands.

I'd not given serious thought to the beer drinking, however, until God asked me the pointed question about my sloppiness as a Christian. I thought of counseling situations God had opened to me and realized that the smell of beer on my breath was not only unpleasant, it wasn't much of a Christian witness, either. So, in answer to God's question, and wanting to please Him, I dropped my beer-drinking immediately.

Unwholesome conversation seemed to be a part of business situations, too. In a previous position God had given me wisdom in handling those who enjoyed telling smutty jokes or using vulgarities. My immediate superior, upon learning I was a Christian, began singing ribald songs about Jesus Christ, using vulgar language and speaking about immoralities. I wanted to counter him. But a voice in me cautioned, "Be still. He doesn't know what he's doing." My silence proved right as I simply continued to act as a Christian.

A few years later, as an executive, I found myself in the same office with this man whose mouth had troubled me. But a change had taken place. There were no more foul songs or language. Instead, I enjoyed his respect as he questioned me about my Christian life. Soon he began his own search for God.

When I became district manager of the Youngstown, Ohio branch of the E. F. McDonald Incentive Company, I replaced a "swinger." The men wondered if my Christian commitment would be a hindrance to my management. However, God blessed me. The business grew, profits increased substantially, and we became the most profitable district in the company. Soon I was profiled on the Dayton sales charts as the model for other salespersons to follow.

Often when my boss, Bob, called me on business from the main office in Dayton he would ask, "How is Jesus Christ and the twelve disciples?" referring to the men under me.

"Jesus is always good and I'm doing good, too," I would usually reply.

The next time he called, upon answering I might hear him singing, in jest, "Rock of ages, cleft for me."

Bob began to respect my convictions, though, and was conscious of my performance. One day he came to Youngstown to discuss business. Just a day or two before I'd been to an ecumenical service at the Jewish Synagogue, where I'd been given a yarmulke, or skull cap, to wear and keep. When Bob visited, the cap was in my desk drawer. During our conversation, as Bob bent over papers, he commented, "Sometimes I think you're Jewish."

At that I reached quietly into my drawer, and when Bob turned I was wearing the skull cap. How we laughed together. It was such incidents that shaped our friendship.

Later, when I'd gone to Chicago as regional manager, then finally to Dayton as marketing manager, our ties grew even stronger.

On my lapel I always wore my Yokefellow pin. One day when I forgot it, Bob exhorted me. "Don't you forget to wear that every day," he scolded. Now he was even asking about certain Bible passages.

When he suddenly died of a heart attack at the age of forty, I felt Bob went believing in Christ.

In 1974, when the corporation closed the division I was in, and when I didn't want to move again, I found myself without a job. At fifty, I knew this could be a serious problem.

"What will you do, Dad?" my oldest boy asked.

"Don't worry, Son," I replied. "God is my Boss and He has some plan for me." I knew Psalm 37:23, "The steps of a good man are ordered by the Lord; and he delighteth in his way." So I was at rest.

"I really have a pulling to go back to New York State," I told June one day.

"That's funny. I've been getting the same feeling," she replied. We stared at each other for several seconds, sensing God had been speaking to both our hearts.

When I let the company know I'd be willing to move, I received immediate offers. One was to Central New York. I accepted, and we landed in Canandaigua — significantly, an Indian name meaning "chosen place." An old farmhouse needing extensive repairs became our new home.

"I believe God has a reason and plan for our getting this place," stated Mary Louise when we moved in. We all agreed.

Later we learned that in 1865 the original owner had spoken prophetically. A Christian, he said the property would always be used to God's glory. His last wish, to be buried on the property, was granted, and his gravestone stands as a reminder that God fulfills His Word.

# Chapter Fourteen

# The Fleece

*"And all things, whatsoever ye shall ask in prayer, believing, ye shall receive"* (Matt. 21:22).

I'd experienced the power of the Holy Spirit in my life from the age of eight. There were special touches, such as the one I'd had in the doctor's office. But I loved to pray and spent much time in prayer. Although other gifts of the Holy Spirit had long been operating through me, the gift of tongues was foreign. I didn't even know anyone who spoke in tongues.

It wasn't until the early seventies that I became acquainted with the Full Gospel Businessmen's Fellowship and the gift of tongues.

Soon afterward, I stood over the book table in a Christian bookstore praying simplistically, "Lord, direct me to the right book." I opened my eyes to find my hand resting on *They Speak with Other Tongues*, a book about the charismatic renewal by John and Elizabeth Sherrill.

I'd not quite finished it when one day, while on a business trip to Buffalo, I began praising the Lord. The intensity of my worship increased until suddenly I was aware that I had no understanding of what I was saying. The language pouring from my lips was something other than English, and I drove around Buffalo praying delightedly in my new tongue. A bubbling sensation filled me as I drove and prayed for two hours.

An appointment couldn't curtail the beautiful experience I was enjoying. While waiting, I hid around a corner in the reception area away from the receptionist, so I could practice this strange new language. Every few minutes I'd come out, smile at her sheepishly, then once more retreat to the corner to pray.

What a wonderful, greater dimension in the Spirit I now sensed! I learned how important praise and worship are to our life in the Spirit.

Prior to this my prayer life was very simple, and I spent much time in meditation and poetry. Now prayer was more alive.

* * * * * * *

I stared out the kitchen window at the birdfeeder I'd put out in January. It had been a Christmas gift from my mother-in-law and we'd excitedly anticipated the many birds we'd see. Now it was three months later as I studied the birdless feeder, filled with the best seed I could buy — guaranteed to attract many varieties of birds. But there were none.

Perhaps it needed stability, I thought, so I added a crosspiece from the feeder over to a nearby tree. Still no results.

The station looked so lonely, standing under gray winter skies, as if its invitation had been rejected.

Suddenly, it occurred to me that I could use this birdfeeder in putting a fleece before the Lord like Gideon did in Judges chapter six. There were two subjects I'd questioned God about that morning: whether to become involved in prison ministry and whether I should join the organization of which I'd recently become aware, the Full Gospel Businessmen's Fellowship International.

I'd attempted to visit prisons through the Yoke-fellow organization when we lived in Ohio, but never could arrange it. As a member of the prison board of Yokefellows, I felt a bit guilty.

Living now in Canandaigua, I'd learned we were situated between two large prisons, Attica and Auburn. I'd wondered if God would open the doors or if He even wanted me in prison ministry. I'd felt, though, that He'd given me Matthew 25:40 — that He was in prison and I should visit Him.

Soon after I'd sensed God's call to prisons, I'd been in Syracuse on business. During that day several people questioned me about the Yokefellow lapel pin. Upon explaining that it signified the yoke of Christ as found in Matthew 11:29, three individuals on separate occasions answered me, "You ought to see Frank Hummel." I knew only that Mr. Hummel was an executive with a corporation with which my company was doing business.

That evening, pondering the events of the day, I flipped the radio dial and suddenly caught words from the Christian Broadcasting Network. I soon found it to be a live broadcast from the Full Gospel Businessmen's Regional Convention in Syracuse. I was thrilled to hear beautiful testimonies of God's love and power.

After several minutes, my excitement heightened as I heard, "And now we introduce Mr. Frank Hummel, President of the Full Gospel Businessmen's Fellowship chapter in Syracuse." With the words I'd received that day fresh in my mind, I knew God would soon bring us together.

My evening's remodeling work seemed unimportant as I perched on a box, hammer in hand, to hear the Catholic priest Frank Hummel had introduced, Father John Bertolucci. Nearly two hours flew by as I listened intently to the recounting of the wonderful things Christ had done in this priest's life. How exciting it was to hear him tell of his experience of the Baptism in the

Holy Spirit! I decided that night that I wanted to become a part of this Full Gospel organization. Now, along with my burning desire to go into prisons, there was this new desire. But I had to know God's leading.

So it was that I stood before the window, gazing at the feeder.

I took stock of myself there, wondering what God had in mind for me. I felt small and limited, questioning if I might be considering involvements beyond my capabilities. Pushing that thought aside was another — that if God was in me, then through Him I could accomplish the purposes He ordained. Since I felt like Gideon, I decided to do what he'd done.

"Lord, I'm going to put this fleece before you," I prayed out loud. "If you want me involved in the Full Gospel Businessmen's Fellowship and prison ministry, put a bird in that feeder right now."

No sooner had the prayer left my lips than, to my delight, a sparrow landed on the crosspiece I'd nailed to the tree. I continued to watch with growing excitement as I saw its feathers bend as if a hand was pushing the bird. It stepped sideways across the board until its tiny legs were firmly buried in the seed all around it. As the sparrow began eating, another flew from the ground, landed beside it, and together they ate for about two minutes, then flew off. Although I watched for the birds to return, they didn't. (How happy we were when, within a week, our feeder became a popular source of food for a great variety of birds!)

Many people say we're not to put a fleece before the Lord. I believe we should hear from the Lord clearly enough that we don't have to constantly ask for a sign or many confirmations. But we must also be sensitive to the Holy Spirit's leading. If we love God and have pure, sincere hearts, then we can ask Him to confirm whatever we believe we've heard, and He will answer.

I soon became a charter member in the newly-formed Full Gospel Businessmen's chapter in

Canandaigua, learning of it through a phone call to Mr. Hummel. I was chosen as vice president and began sharing my testimony at various chapter meetings. God was developing my sensitivity to His Spirit as I saw Him touch many people — saving, healing and baptizing them in His Holy Spirit.

# Chapter Fifteen

# F. G. B. M. F. I.

*"But ye shall receive power, after that the Holy Ghost is come upon you..."* (Acts 1:8)

I'd learned the name of the chaplain at Auburn Prison in Auburn, New York, and had decided to give him a call.

"My name's Jack Moore and I'm part of the national Yokefellows," I began, then explained my desire to visit the prison.

"Isn't this something!" Burt Nussey replied when I reached him. "I was just praying that someone would call who was familiar with Yokefellows."

We met and I began visiting Auburn Prison on Saturdays to see if the men would accept me. When I wanted to establish an evening service once a week, I learned there were no nights available. It was time for prayer. Immediately God opened up Friday nights.

The first thing I learned as I started ministering in Auburn Prison was that no matter what crimes these men had committed, God accepted and loved them. The initial small group grew over the weeks as we shared the good news of Jesus Christ.

One evening we all sensed that God planned to do

something special, so we began to pray. In a few moments a prisoner came forward asking for prayer that a scar on his face be removed. The Lord told me that I was to pray instead for him to be filled with the Holy Spirit so that he'd lose his awareness of the scar. I began to pray and immediately the power of the Lord fell on this man. He was filled with the Holy Spirit and began praying in a new language. Another prisoner came forward and had a similar experience. One by one, the Christian prisoners came for prayer and fell because of the greatness of God's power as He anointed them with His Spirit. Several men were delivered from demons, then filled with the Holy Spirit and given a heavenly language.

We wondered how the guards would react, for the first guard had run to get a sergeant. The sergeant, in turn, hurried to get a lieutenant, and they all peered at us through the large window from the hallway outside. One inmate stood by the door, hands folded in prayer as he asked God to give the guards understanding.

I later learned that in a maximum security institution, if someone is "out" on the floor, a full written report must be submitted stating the reason. Sixteen men lay on the floor that night under God's power, but no questions were asked. And no report was written, for which we praised the Lord.

Chaplain Nussey and I had become fast friends.

"Do you pray in tongues?" I asked this Methodist one day. "No," was his quick reply. So I bagged one of my favorite books on the subject of the baptism in the Holy Spirit and gave it to him.

Three months went by and he'd not yet read the book.

One day, while taking care of some business near his home, I decided to call Burt. He suggested I stop in for coffee.

I'd been impressed by his quiet, imperturbable manner. His gentle warmth was a testimony to all those around him. Today was no different.

Coffee wasn't enough. He insisted we have breakfast, so the aroma of scrambled eggs and bacon filled the kitchen.

Suddenly Burt turned to me. "I suppose you've got to want the Holy Spirit and tongues to come into it," he said, both a statement and a question. I nodded.

"What Scripture do you give people when you tell them about this?" he asked further.

Since this was prior to my ministering the Baptism in the Holy Spirit in prison, I'd not yet led anyone into the experience. So I wasn't sure what I'd say to a seeker. While getting my Bible from the car, I had some time to think.

"You're going to seem foolish," my mind taunted.

I opened my Bible to the concordance and looked under "tongues." There in bold letters I saw "I Cor. 4:10." Quickly I turned to the reference. "We are fools for Christ's sake," I read. My heart pounded and I knew I had to answer this friend whose opinion I valued. Turning back to the concordance, I was astonished to find the black, bold letters listing First Corinthians 4:10 gone! Then I began hearing the voice within. "Don't push the Spirit. Don't shove the Dove."

Burt looked at me with spiritual hunger in his eyes when I returned to the kitchen.

"Jack, will you pray with me?" he asked, as he knelt in front of the picture window in his living room. My only thought was of the people who could easily see us kneeling and hear us praying aloud like Daniel. However, I knew my courage was no match for his.

"Lord, how do I pray?" I wondered. But I needn't have asked, for just as I reached out to lay my hands on Burt's head and said, "Jesus, I love you," he began praying in another language. Tears streamed down our faces and I fell to my knees. Together we began to loudly sing our praises to God.

Then, uncharacteristically, Burt and I began praising and dancing like playful children around his living room. By this time, delighted with what I knew God was doing, I cared little if the whole town had turned out to peer in at the strange happenings in my friend's living room.

****

The first meeting of the Full Gospel Businessmen's Fellowship International in Canandaigua was held in 1974 at the home of Gib Buckbee. It seemed so wonderful to get together with men who were seeking the Lord and making plans to establish an FGBMFI chapter.

We prayed and sang together, then various men began to share their testimonies. This was the first time I'd met Dick Toulson. When he told of laying his hands on his refrigerator and praying for the motor to work, within myself I said, "Aw, come on now. Why would God want to do those things when we're totally capable of doing them ourselves? Why in the world did He give us two arms and two legs and the ability to use a pair of pliers and a screwdriver? Why did He give us the Maytag repairman?"

There was no question in my mind, after the experiences I'd had over the years, that God could do anything He wanted. But to pray for these things seemed a bit questionable. Fortunately, when we have a weak area, but are sincerely seeking God, He'll allow us an experience just to give us a revelation of Himself and develop our faith.

That's what He seemed to be doing with me for a while in 1975. Twice I felt guided to pray about car problems — windshield wipers that had refused to work and a burned-out cruise control system. After prayer, both the wipers and cruise control worked just fine.

The week following my experience with the cruise control, I was on a business trip. As I entered a four-lane highway and was rejoicing in the Lord, I felt so full of faith and wonder at His glorious power that a confession burst from my lips: "Lord, I believe I could lay my hands on an automobile that was stalled by the road and it would start, because I feel Your Presence so strongly!"

I wondered at myself and my strange words as I studied the highway ahead of me. Suddenly I spied a car pulled off along the highway, hood up.

"Oh, no! Now what have I said?" was my next thought. "Was that me speaking, Lord, or was it You speaking through me?" My faith waned rapidly.

I slowed the car a bit and noticed a lady behind the wheel of the stalled vehicle; but I drove past, knowing I should have stopped. I was sure God was testing me.

I tried arguing with Him. "But Lord, this is a four-lane highway with a divider in the middle, and there's no way now that I can go back."

Suddenly, as if God had just then put it in place, there was a crossover. Now I knew for certain there was no escaping.

As I headed in the opposite direction, watching for another crossover, I prayed nervously. "God, if You want to get that car started before I get there, that will be wonderful, and I'll just know that You're able to do those things. So it's all right with me if that car's gone."

All too soon I'd driven the four miles to another crossover and saw the car ahead. I slowed, then stopped, not really knowing what to do.

"Do you know what the problem is?" I asked the lady. She had no idea; maybe water in the carburetor, she suggested. "The car just won't start," she told me.

I inquired about her battery, which she said was fine.

"Lord, what do I do?" I quickly asked. "Maybe You just want me to use whatever ingenuity I have to get this car started."

Knowing my limited expertise regarding car engines, I was certain I wouldn't get far. Taking off the air cleaner seemed a good thing to do. Maybe I could wiggle some parts and make something happen. But nothing moved.

"Try it now," I instructed the woman. Still no results. There was only the whirr of an engine trying to turn over.

I knew what my mission was, my purpose in being here. God had already shown me through the other experiences that He was able to do ALL that we asked, if we asked in faith. It was time, I knew, to act on that faith. Being well-hidden from the lady's view, I laid my hands on the carburetor.

"In the Name of Jesus Christ, start. And I'll give You all the praise and glory."

"Try it now," I told her. As she turned the key, we heard the beautiful sound of a well-running engine.

"Do I dare take my fingers off this carburetor?" I wondered next. But the engine continued purring with no hesitation. I returned the air cleaner to its place and tightened the wing nut.

"Do you know how I got the car started?" I asked her as I stuck my head through the open window on the passenger's side.

"I guess you're just a good mechanic," she replied.

"I'm not a mechanic at all. I don't know anything about automobiles," I explained. "The Lord led me to stop and pray over this car."

I noted her widening eyes as her jaw dropped.

"Jesus Christ can do anything He wants to do," I continued.

She kept staring. Then I realized that this experience was for me, not her. Pulling my head from the window, I went back to the front of the car and closed the hood with a bang. The woman hardly allowed me enough time to jump clear before zooming off down the highway. I grinned, wondering how she'd explain to someone that a man laid his hands on her car and said Jesus started it.

# Chapter Sixteen

# In the Jungle

*"...But with God all things are possible"* (Matt. 19:26).

With God giving me the three former experiences within three weeks, I realized He was still teaching me to trust Him in everything.

The fourth week I found myself traveling with two men, Dick Smith and Dick Patterson, both executives in air-conditioning companies. We were examining possible vacation sites for those in their companies who had earned travel awards.

The Condodora Island in Panama, where the Shah of Iran had stayed, was one of our stops. We had a great time, with good accommodations and good food. Then we headed for Puerto Viarta, Mexico, and checked at our hotel for entertainment ideas.

After our first day I learned of a jungle trip and asked our trip director if such a jaunt could be arranged. Before we'd finished our lunch in one of the local restaurants, the director found me.

"I have a guide out front to take you into the jungle," he excitedly said.

I explained that Dick Smith had to catch a plane for

another point in Mexico at six p.m., so we'd have to be back by then.

"Oh, it won't be any problem," he assured me. "This man knows the jungle, and he's going to take you right now."

With lunch unfinished, we grabbed this opportunity for some excitement.

In front of the hotel sat a pathetic yellow taxicab.

"Don't we need a four-wheel jeep for the jungle?" I quickly asked.

"No, not necessary," replied the driver, Poncho, in broken English.

"He knows the roads and can get you there and back in good time," the director reiterated.

With a degree of apprehension, I got into the front seat while the two Dicks climbed in back, and off we wheezed.

My fears were first confirmed when Poncho had to stop to ask for directions not far up the highway. Everything was all right, he assured me, after I questioned him in my limited Spanish. He knew the way. Finally, he found a road which headed down into the jungle.

By that time we'd noticed that every time the taxi's speed exceeded sixty, up would fly the hood. I feared it would rip through the windshield. But Poncho, undaunted, stopped each time and relatched it with a grin as if this were the most common occurrence in the world.

Poncho also had the curious habit of looking in our direction while babbling in Spanish, thus running off the side of the road. I'd yell so he could quickly pull the taxi back into our lane.

The road soon was nothing more than an unimproved path as we headed into the deepening jungle. To make it worse, it was the dry time of year and white dust filled the narrow path. Glancing back at my friends, I saw four dark eyes peering through dust-covered faces

as if they had just popped up from flour barrels.
Embarrassed, I accepted their friendly gibes about my
idea of an experienced jungle guide.

A stream lay ahead, but Poncho, without slowing the
taxi, splashed through to the other side. The engine
began to ping severely as we continued.

Suddenly there was a junction — a mere convergence
of narrow paths. A hut stood on one corner. Poncho
stopped, disappeared into the tiny structure, and finally, after several minutes, reappeared. Heading off in
a different direction, we continued on our jungle
journey. It was quite evident by now that we were
thoroughly lost. I was feeling the responsibility for
getting these men back to the hotel on time while
providing them with a certain degree of entertainment.
So far, the most interesting things we'd seen were a
bunch of wild cows, thick jungle trees and a Mexican on
an ambling donkey.

As we headed down the middle of one path, there in
front of us sat the burned-out, rusted skeleton of a
Buick.

"Let's stop here, Jack, and you get a picture of us
sitting in that old car," one of the men suggested. "It'll
help you redeem this trip."

"That will make an interesting picture," was the
bland statement I weakly mumbled as I contemplated
our predicament.

Poncho pulled off the road to one side of the burned
car and shut off the engine. Carefully the men eased
themselves into the old frame. After a few moments of
picture-taking, we climbed back into the taxi.

Poncho turned the key. Nothing. Out we crawled,
threw up the hood and wiggled some wires. Still
nothing. No sound at all.

We checked the battery. Not a drop of water was in it.

"New battery," Poncho said.

"New battery, but no water," one Dick spoke.

We had no tools, not that it would have mattered

with a dead battery, but it seemed to emphasize the hopelessness of our desperate situation.

"Here we are lost in the middle of the jungle," I thought, "And Dick Smith has to be at the airport before six o'clock." I was frantic as I visualized us sleeping in the jungle with our lives in jeopardy.

Not knowing what else to do, I walked up the road a short ways, stepped off into some bushes and cried out to the Lord.

"What do I do to get these men back?" I pleaded.

"I'll start the car," I heard the voice say clearly, as if a radio were planted out here in the middle of nowhere. I was so thankful that God had prepared me with the previous experiences.

Without hesitating, I quickly returned to the car and ordered the men to get in.

"It's going to start," I announced.

Poncho, Dick Smith and Dick Patterson all obeyed while I hid behind the hood to lay my hands on the battery.

"In the Name of Jesus, start!" I commanded. "All right, Poncho."

He turned the key and immediately the engine responded. I slammed the hood, feeling great that God had once again proven Himself to be "a very present help in trouble."

"Now I want you to share with these two men what I have done," was God's next directive.

In my head I argued with Him, reminding Him that it's not good to throw a pearl before swine, as if He didn't know. Not that I was belittling my friends. But I knew my explanation would tax the limits of their spiritual understanding.

One of the men had his Master's degree from Syracuse University, I told God, and the other had six years at Harvard. These were thinking men, not ones with whom I could share something like this. "They won't understand," I told Him.

"DO IT!" the firm voice answered.

As I'd traveled around the country with Dick Smith, I'd shared with him many of the wonderful things God had done for me. He'd been fascinated, but this was something pretty wild. Nevertheless, I began.

"Men, do you know how I started the car?" I asked, as if they could have an idea about what I'd done.

"No, tell us," they said eagerly.

"Jesus Christ actually started the car."

Dick Smith jumped, hitting his head on the roof of the taxi.

"Jesus Christ doesn't start cars!" he yelled in protest.

A half-hour theological discussion ensued, while Poncho somehow managed to get us out of the jungle and on our way back to town.

"You have more things happening to you than Jesus Christ had happening to Him," said one of the fellows.

It was a perfect opportunity to explain that although only fifty-seven miracles are recorded in Scripture, John's Gospel tells us that it would take more books than could fill the earth if all the wonderful things Jesus did were written down.

But I went on to tell them that Jesus said, "Greater things than these shall he [the believer] do; because I go unto My Father." I further explained that anything that's done is accomplished by Jesus, even today, because He's the same, yesterday, today and forever; that through the power of His Holy Spirit we are able to do those works in His Name that will bring glory to Him.

"How would you have gotten us out of the jungle?" I asked as we neared the close of our discussion. They had no idea.

I was glad I could tell them that God was interested in helping His servant and those for whom he was responsible — that God Himself was interested in getting us out of the jungle.

I delivered Dick Smith back to town, shaken and dust-covered, but safe and in time to catch his plane.

That evening, as Dick Patterson and I shared dinner, he said, "Surely Someone planned this day. It didn't just happen."

I concurred.

# Chapter Seventeen

# Commissioned

*"Now thanks be unto God, which always causeth us to triumph in Christ, and maketh manifest the savour of his knowledge by us in every place"* (II Cor. 2:14).

Along with my involvement in FGBMFI and prison ministry, I became more committed to witnessing for the Lord in business.

"Who's been saved by Jack today?" a client asked my secretary, who, interpreting it negatively, promptly reported the remark to my boss. Quickly he made a trip to Rochester to warn me that if I continued to "witness," I was in danger of being fired.

Interestingly, my client had asked me many questions about the Lord. My answers had satisfied him and, as a result, he'd taken his family and rejoined the Catholic Church. Often he asked me what the Lord was doing in my life and encouraged me to put my experiences into print.

To alleviate my boss' fears, I assured him that I would not force my faith on anyone, not initiating conversations, but would only be responsive to inquiries, sensitive to the Holy Spirit. I endeavored to explain in terms I thought he could understand. However, I boldly stated that I had to give witness when asked. After a further gentle reprimand, he left.

Prophecies of an outpouring of God's Spirit in the Rochester area, even over New York State and throughout the east coast began drifting in from various places. "You're going to be a part of this," I heard in my spirit. And I asked repeatedly, "Really, Lord? Am I?" The feeling of inadequacy flooded over me as in the past.

Often I was invited to speak at FGBMFI meetings, and the prison ministry had expanded. Over thirty men were gathering in the Friday night prison services.

In prison I met one of the residents who asked me to see his friend, Jo Teske. Knowing what God was doing in the prison, she desired to have a teaching and ministry group in her home. We expanded and moved to the Good News Bookstore. God was doing many marvelous things and we started to keep a record of those. But He instructed us not to do that. He'd keep the records, He said.

When the group grew to nearly twenty, we were crowding the walls of the little bookshop. We needed a bigger building and asked God to provide one.

Two Salvation Army soldiers came to one meeting. They started to run out, however, when people began falling to the floor under the Holy Spirit's anointing. Suddenly, an angel appeared and blocked the doorway. The soldiers fell and immediately were baptized in the Holy Spirit.

The two soldiers later approached their leader, Captain Whitacre, affectionately called "Cap," to ask if we could use their building. We began holding the meetings in the Salvation Army Citadel.

Although we didn't advertise, the number soon rose to over sixty, then to more than eighty. The Captain watched his people come in and get filled with the Holy Spirit. His own congregation suddenly grew from about ten to thirty-five. People were getting excited about Jesus and His work in their lives. Puzzled at the change taking place in his church members, "Cap" joined us to see what was going on.

I'd been teaching on Jesus, the Christ. One evening after I finished my teaching, about sixty people joined in a circle for prayer in the back of the chapel. "Cap" watched and listened as people fell under God's power. He said nothing, but left to seek God on his knees, alone.

"God, I don't believe this is of You," he stated. "This has got to be Satan. I've never seen anything like it," he continued. "I'm going back to that meeting next week, but You've got to show me if this man's of God or if he's of Satan. If he's of Satan, I'll kick him out. I'm going to put him to the test."

The next week, there was "Cap" in uniform. He was the first to come for prayer.

"Oh, so you've come to test God?" I asked, looking into his eyes. (He told me this later, since I didn't remember.)

He also says, "I heard, 'In the Name of Jesus,' as I closed my eyes." When he opened them, thinking he still stood, how surprised he was to look up from the floor. He received the baptism in the Holy Spirit that night, speaking in tongues when he opened his eyes the second time.

The next week his wife met me at the door. "I want it right now," she said.

"What do you want?" I asked.

"The same thing my husband has — the Holy Spirit."

"I'll pray for you after the service," I offered, thinking of all those in the chapel waiting for the meeting to start.

"No, I want it now," she stated firmly.

I prayed a simple prayer and out she went on the concrete floor, praying in a new tongue.

A soldier stood nearby. "I want the same thing," he

said. I prayed for him, too. He went out in the Spirit and lay by the chapel door.

Half an hour later, friends helped the Captain's wife into the meeting, seating her beside someone she'd not liked. Now, though, all wrong feelings had melted and been replaced by God's love.

The Whitacre's ministry changed and their congregation grew to over one hundred.

There are those who disagree with people "falling out" in the Spirit during times of prayer. Many call it being "slain in the Spirit." I dislike the term only because it doesn't seem to fit with Scripture. I know that many in the Bible fell to the ground under God's power — Daniel fell before the Lord when the Angel of the Lord came before him.

In the Gospel of John, those who came to take Jesus fell before Him as He stepped forward. So, I accepted what I saw happening and rejected only the semantics.

At an FGBMFI Advance, God confirmed through some of the men what He'd already told me — "You have been given the gift of healing."

I was satisfied that God was using His gifts through me to build and establish His Kingdom. But I was also satisfied with my work and the company benefits. It was my satisfaction that left me totally unprepared for the next experience God had for me.

*******

I looked at the clock. Six a.m. I knew it was the voice of the Lord that had awakened me. Clearly He'd instructed me to get up and go to the "upper room," a large room we had set aside for prayer in the upper story of the house.

Quietly I slipped out of bed so as not to awaken June. I quickly realized it was our anniversary, June 14, 1977. But that wasn't the cause for the anticipation I felt at the moment.

With each step toward the upper room I sensed an

increasing Presence, as if I were walking in the very steps of Jesus Himself. My heart asked, "Is this the way it was, Jesus, when You went to be alone with the Father? Am I really walking in Your steps?"

I lowered myself to the sofa bed and softly began to pray. Suddenly I felt my body falling forward. I knew I could stop what was happening; but a voice seemed to say, "Don't stop this. Be sensitive to what the Spirit is showing you."

As I obeyed the spiritual instinct, I found myself lying flat on my back, arms outstretched and one foot over the arch of the other.

Although by now I'd seen many people fall under the Spirit's anointing as I prayed for them, never had I experienced God's power in this way.

Then I heard what seemed to be an audible voice. It was clear and precise. The Lord spoke many things to me about ministry and what I'd be doing. His anointing, He said, would be on my life from that moment on.

Next I heard a strange request. "I want you to start speaking the names of all the men and women you know whom you feel have dedicated their lives to me."

Several names quickly came to mind. But more strange than the request was my inability to speak them. With the remembrance of each name and my attempt to speak, I heard, "Go on to the next." Finally, after several such attempts, my lips were loosed as another person sprang into thought. This continued for some time until I had named three persons.

"Those whom you could name are those who can believe with you for the impossible miracles which I will do," I heard the Holy Spirit speak. "Permit no one else to lay hands on people you're praying for in these impossible situations, but only those I have given you," He continued. "As time goes by, I will give you new names as those people enter into the proper belief."

Later, through experience, I learned that when people who didn't fully believe in divine healing laid their hands on someone, their unbelief hindered the effectiveness of the prayer. At times I have gently removed another's hands from someone. Other times I've been led to have someone else come and lay their hands on a person, sensing their complete faith in God's power.

Although at times my actions have caused misunderstandings, I'm thankful that since God spoke to me, there are more and more Christians who believe in God's miracles. He's bringing many into ministry in His Spirit.

At seven o'clock God concluded speaking with these words: "Now you can confirm My call upon your life by My Word."

My mind's reply was, "But I didn't bring a Bible with me." As if in answer, my head was forcefully turned to the left where I saw my pocket Bible lying next to my hand. Ordinarily it wouldn't stay open by itself. But this morning, there it was, held open. Quickly I stood, took the Bible into the light from the window and immediately began to read from John 15, verses sixteen through nineteen, Jesus' charge to His disciples: "Ye have not chosen Me, I have chosen you. The world will hate you, for it first hated Me."

I recalled words from Paul's first letter to the Corinthians: "I came before you in fear and trembling." He had been humbled in His encounter with Jesus Christ, from intellectualism to a single, direct message: "Jesus Christ and Him crucified." Paul had added that he would come in demonstration of power — the power of the Holy Ghost.

I'd already had evidence of that same power in my life. Sometimes it seemed overwhelming. But now I realized God was making a new call on me.

A short time later God spoke to me again. "Now I want you to be ordained and enter into full-time ministry for Me. You're to resign from your position with the corporation, give up Social Security, drop your hospitalization plans, and you are to trust fully in Me."

I had a choice to make. I'd just been given two offers, one of which would ultimately lead me into the position of president of a division. I was faced with the opportunity to make more money than ever before.

But God's call was on my life.

"God, give me something from your Scriptures to confirm Your call," I prayed.

As I opened the Word to the Gospel of Luke and read Satan's temptation of Jesus, "Bow down and worship me and I will give You all the kingdoms of the world," I knew what I had to do.

In a meeting with my superiors in New York, I handed in my resignation. Just prior to this, I'd been licensed by Elim Fellowship in Lima, New York and was scheduled for ordination. I knew God's hand was upon my life, and His timing was perfect.

Wise counsel must be sought by those who desire full-time ministry. I see people giving up jobs and families, suffering with unpaid bills, while believing God has called them into ministry. If it's God's call, He will confirm His Word by meeting every need and opening the doors.

Of course, there may be some obstacles to test our faith. However, God gives a peace in those circumstances. We don't have to struggle, knocking down walls.

God has met every need since we've gone into the ministry and "lived by faith." A ministry that began in a small church in Auburn, New York and another starting in a chicken coop in Canandaigua, New York, now have world-wide outreaches. God indeed has confirmed His Word.

In a Sunday morning prayer meeting, as I was thanking God for using small works, a word of rebuke came. "Don't call anything I have started 'small,' " the Lord spoke through one of the church elders.

Most of my adult life so far had been spent serving Jesus Christ as a "layman," teaching the Word, conducting weekly Koinonia Yokefellow meetings in our home and filling pulpits here and there. God needs the engineers, the plumbers and the farmers. He needs people employed in the world to be a witness wherever they go. He knows our hearts, our abilities, and it's He who does the choosing. He would have us serve Him and be ministers wherever we find ourselves. After all, it's not sacrifice God's looking for, but our obedience.

\*\*\*

# Chapter Eighteen

# More Ministry in Auburn

*"...I will pour out my spirit upon all flesh ... and also upon the servants and upon the handmaids in those days will I pour out my spirit"* (Joel 2:28,29).

I was despondent one day as I drove from Syracuse, New York, where I'd been on business. A secretary I knew was dying of cancer, and I'd felt I should go pray for her. Another secretary had encouraged me, saying her friend would appreciate my visit.

After two hours of searching, I'd found the woman's home, but was met at the door by a member of the family. As I stood outside, word of my arrival was sent upstairs to the sick woman. However, she refused to see me.

"Who am I, Lord, to say I'd come pray for her?" I asked dejectedly as I got back into my car. "How can I be so presumptuous? She wouldn't even let me in the house and she's going to die. What is all this?" I drove on, mulling over the rejection I felt.

Approaching Auburn, I decided to stop at a restaurant near the prison, thinking a good meal might perk my sagging self-esteem. How surprised I was to find Jo Teske there with a young woman visiting from Denver.

Jo had just prayed, "Lord, please send Jack Moore."
But this was a Thursday, a day I was never in Auburn.

The girl with Jo had arthritic hands and was unable
to write without pain. Jo had shared Scriptures, preparing her to receive healing. It was even more surprising that God chose the moment I walked through
the door to heal her.

Jo sat trembling. "You've got to pray for me," she
said, and immediately went out in the Spirit. Her neck
was twisted around and pinned between the wall and
the chair for seven minutes. Fortunately, no other
customers were there. I explained to the girl what had
happened, since she was unfamiliar with such demon-
strations of God's power.

"Lord, if a waitress or customers come in, what are
they going to think?" was the prayer running through
my mind. "Please keep them out," I asked. And no one
came.

Finally, Jo came to. "I had a bad neck when I went
down," she said, excitedly. "But the pain's all gone. I
feel wonderful."

Now other customers came and the waitress returned. We left for the Christian bookstore next door
where others joined us in prayer. The girl from Denver
later received Jesus and was baptized in the Holy
Spirit. A few years later she expressed in a letter her
continuing walk with the Lord.

I was glad God had taken my despondency and
turned it into rejoicing. I was reminded, too, that
though some refuse His intervention in their lives,
there will always be those who welcome Him.

During one day of ministry in Auburn, Jo Teske and
I witnessed to a young Catholic woman. Jo had met her
at Auburn Prison while both were visiting inmates. It
wasn't unusual for Jo to find someone to witness to and
take to her home.

"I'd like to have the joy you two have," the woman
said as we visited.

"You can," I assured her, after sharing the Lord for several minutes. One of the women suggested we eat before further discussion and prayer. I offered to treat the ladies to supper at a nearby place. However, as we looked over the menus, a sinking feeling washed over me as I remembered I had only twelve dollars in my pocket.

"Lord, please guide us all on how to order," I quickly prayed. When the bill came, I breathed more easily. I'd have one dollar left over, even after the tip.

Back at Jo's house I silently prayed, "Lord, don't let her see a man; let her see Jesus."

Before we ministered to her again, she said, "I really want to see Jesus." In acknowledging Christ as her Savior, the young woman began to exhibit her new-found excitement.

"I see the hands of Christ on me," she soon shared, and began dancing around the room, displaying the joy she'd wanted.

Then it was time to head home. Suddenly I saw the gas gauge. It registered empty. Only a dollar was left in my wallet, I recalled. I opened it anyway. Much to my astonishment, there was another twelve dollars. I used the miracle money for gas and happily started for home.

When I arrived, I found a dividend check for twenty dollars in the mail. "This is Your money, Lord," I spoke, and placed it on my bureau.

The next day I headed out of my office for lunch. Then I remembered I'd spent all my funds on gasoline the night before. I'd have to stop at the bank and cash a check. Almost unconsciously, however, I pulled my wallet from my back pocket. Opening it, I found, to my great surprise, another twelve dollars. The corner of still another piece of money peeked from behind those. It was twenty dollars.

"Thank you, Lord," I said, laughing, and shook my head in childlike wonder.

God had done a similar thing for June and me when we lived in Youngstown, Ohio, proving He provides well for His children.

During the years I had cancer, funds were tight. We owed a local service station $162 for gas and oil and were unable to pay the bill.

"Lord, we don't want to be delinquent," we prayed. We wanted to demonstrate our integrity as Christians by paying our bill on time.

The day after our prayer, a check came in the mail. It was a bonus award from the company. The amount was $155.

"That's not quite enough, Lord, but I sure do appreciate it," I spoke with a smile. Just then, as I carried the check and envelope to the kitchen table, another check drifted to the floor. How excited we were to see it was for seven dollars!

We didn't delay in paying our account. And because we'd paid it on time, we received a two-dollar discount.

"Lord, you not only paid our bill, but you gave us a rebate," I said, and thanked Him again for His goodness.

# Chapter Nineteen

# God Teaches How to Be Great

*"But he that is greatest among you shall be your servant"* (Matt. 23:11).

As the years went by, June became more involved with me in the ministry. However, she had difficulty accepting my extended travels and the many hours devoted to teaching and preaching. With a home and children to care for, she couldn't be with me. She wasn't even sure she wanted to be with me on such trips.

In 1977 at a Full Gospel Businessmen's Advance, God spoke and told me that He was anointing me for even greater ministry. As I knelt, weeping before the Lord, my first thought was, "Oh dear God, what will my wife do now?"

"I don't even want you speaking to your wife about Me," I heard God say. "I will bring her to where I want her."

I was surprised at the words, not sure I understood; but I also felt relieved, realizing that God, not I, was responsible for her walk with Him.

I obeyed. No longer did I try to talk with June about

the Lord. I knew I was only to walk, not talk — letting her see Jesus by my life.

Our elder daughter had received the baptism of the Holy Spirit and she and I were enjoying close, intense fellowship. June was hungering, I saw, as she witnessed this relationship. I was reminded of Jesus' words in Matthew 5:6 — that those who hungered and thirsted after righteousness would be filled. It was a promise and I rested on it.

I'd often turned June off by all my talking. I'd suggest she should have been where I was, and to her that was a put down. I hadn't realized what I was doing. Now that God had told me to be quiet, I'd see how He could work when we turn a person over to Him.

Often, we not only hinder our loved ones by our zealousness, we interfere with what God is trying to do in their lives.

Although I couldn't speak with June, I spent much time in prayer, interceding for her. I prayed she'd come into the fulness of the Spirit and experience the same joy I had.

I didn't know that God had arranged a whole series of circumstances and a perfect time to accomplish His purposes in June's life.

Meanwhile, I had to make a trip to San Francisco with other company executives.

The first evening we all met at The Fisherman's Wharf for dinner. As the waiter approached with the pre-dinner wine, I heard, "Your lips are not to touch wine." Although I'd given up other alcohol, I hadn't given wine a thought.

"Oh no, Lord. You know how my boss feels about this. He already thinks I'm peculiar," I countered in my head. But I turned over my glass, wanting to be obedient to God's command.

"What's the matter with you, Jack? How come you're not having any wine?" my boss asked immediately. "Is this another of your Christian ideas?"

I could sense his anger, and my brief remark about not wanting any tonight didn't seem to satisfy him.

The following night we were to eat at one of the finest restaurants in San Francisco. I waited for a call. None came. When I found one of the party, he explained that plans had changed. Still later, another of the group informed me that the executives had already left for the original destination.

I retreated to my room with hurt feelings. But after telling the Lord it was all right, that I understood how I'd make them feel uneasy by not drinking, I decided to enjoy a meal in the hotel's dining room. I'd tucked a Christian booklet into one of my jacket pockets, and as I read and ate, it seemed the Lord Himself was hosting this dinner.

Upon returning to my room, suddenly I fell to my knees under a powerful anointing of His Spirit and began to pray in what sounded like an Oriental language. It was different from any tongue I'd prayed in before. Through interpretation, I knew I was interceding for all the large cities of the world. I sensed the corruption, sin and immorality. I sensed too, however, that God, by His Holy Spirit, was reaching out to these cities. I'd never had such an experience before and was so glad I'd been spared the executives' company so I could enjoy the Presence of the Lord in a new way.

The next evening, while out walking, I stumbled into a homosexual community and was approached and propositioned by a gaudily-frocked man. I was repulsed, but understood my intercession of the night before. Surrounded by the smothering forces of evil, I realized some of the horrible sin gripping our nation.

The following day, God arranged another test on the wine issue as I lunched with the president and assistant of our company's California branch. The place they'd chosen specialized in wines.

"Now, Jack, in this place you MUST sample the wine. It's excellent!" the president said with a grin.

I felt more boldness since he wasn't my superior. "No, I can't do that," I said with a steady gaze. "My Christian convictions won't permit me to indulge any more. The Lord's told me I can't."

He pressed me no further.

Soon I was on my way home. June planned to meet me in Syracuse, where we'd spend the night. Then I'd see a client the next day before we returned to Canandaigua.

As I prepared to call on my client the next morning, a book fell from my suitcase. *Face Up with a Miracle* was an exciting recounting by a minister, Don Basham, of his life-changing encounter with the Holy Spirit. Before heading out the door, I briefly commented to June that the book was interesting reading.

Near noon I was back. June hurried to the bathroom to finish getting ready for lunch while I stepped to the picture window, raised my hands and began to pray in the Spirit.

"I want you to ask your wife about the Holy Spirit," I heard Him say.

"Lord, You don't want me talking to my wife about You," I argued quietly.

"Do it!"

I stood in front of the bathroom door, wondering why I'd now been commanded to speak to June.

As the door opened, I looked directly at her. "God has told me to ask you about the Holy Spirit."

Tears began to fill her eyes, spilling down her cheeks as her gaze met mine. "I've got it! I've got it!" she cried, as we tightly embraced. We stood crying together while she explained how, after I'd left, she'd picked up the book and turned to the back. There she'd found instructions on receiving the baptism of the Holy Spirit. She had closed her eyes and suddenly a beautiful sweet fragrance like my after-shave lotion, she said, had filled the room. With her eyes still closed, as she continued to meditate, a strange warmth flowed through her body. She then began to speak in what she described as a Hebrew-like tongue.

We enjoyed a lunch together in the downstairs dining room, holding hands under the table while weeping through the entire meal. It was a most unusual time.

I was convinced that had I not been obedient in San Francisco when God instructed me not to touch the wine, He couldn't have worked as He did in June's life that day.

Since then June, as a pastor's wife, has been a great blessing. She travels with me, quietly assisting as I pray for the sick. I greatly admire her adherence to truth and integrity as we minister.

**\* \* \* \***

I was ready to leave Auburn after an evening of home ministry. Glancing at my watch, I saw it was ten o'clock. I'd be back in Canandaigua soon after eleven.

"Let's pray," I suggested in closing as we stood together in the dim light of the kitchen. As I finished a brief prayer of thanks, a brilliant light filled the small room, so bright I couldn't open my eyes. I thought of Heaven's dazzling light as described by the prophet Isaiah.

It seemed we stood for ten minutes, hands raised in worship and adoration, while our voices extolled the Lord. In His euphoric Presence, we were bathed in love.

Then, as the light faded, God spoke. "I am coming soon to fulfill all I have said," He reminded me.

Now we were free to open our eyes. How astounded I was to see it was one a.m. For three hours we'd worshiped in the beautiful light of God's Presence. And our arms weren't the least bit tired. He'd strengthened us, as well.

If His glory is this wonderful on earth, I considered

during my drive home, how much more wonderful His reality will be in Heaven!

**＊＊＊＊**

*"Then a cloud covered the tent of the congregation, and the glory of the Lord filled the tabernacle"* (Ex. 40:34).

"Go and pray."

I'd heard the command many times when God wanted to teach or show me something significant. Today was no different.

Kneeling, I went on my back in the Spirit. Although conscious, I couldn't move. But I felt something strange in my right hand. I squeezed and knew I was gripping a staff.

A cloud began filling the room until I could no longer see the walls. There I was, alone in the cloud, enjoying the holiness of His Spirit while clutching the invisible rough staff.

"Servant" was the word which came to mind. I thought of Moses, God's servant, and his staff.

"You are my servant," I heard and was overwhelmed.

Suddenly, the cloud disappeared. But a great peace remained. The God of Abraham, Isaac, and Jacob is still at work, I thought. Then David's words came to mind. "What is man that thou art mindful of him?" Who am I that You're mindful of me? I wondered.

During prison ministry a few days later, a pastor friend approached me. "Jack, God has a Word for you, he said.

"My son, you are a servant as Moses was a servant," the pastor spoke, knowing nothing of the vision I'd had just days before. "The path you travel will become narrow as if you are walking on an I-beam. I have removed the handrails, and now you must depend on Me for protection and guidance. Look straight ahead to Me. Look not to the right or left. Know that I will not leave you nor forsake you. Your walk will be more difficult."

More than ever, I determined to serve in love wherever God would lead me.

**＊＊＊＊**

I planned to announce my resignation as an officer from FGBMFI at the next general meeting. It was a hard thing to do, since I was convinced of the importance of this businessmen's organization. It's a laymen's ministry. But with the call God had given me to leave the business world and enter full-time ministry, I could no longer retain the officer's position I'd held nearly four years.

We gathered for the home meeting and conducted the necessary business before a time of sharing and prayer. Then we joined hands. As we began to pray, God's power was so strong that I fell on my back under His anointing. As two of the brothers prayed quietly over me, the Lord spoke clearly that I was to kiss their feet.

"Which man, Lord?" I asked.

The directive was plain. "All of them."

"Yes, all right, Lord. I understand. I'll do it," I replied to His clear instructions. As soon as I agreed to obey, I was released to stand. I asked each man to remove his right shoe and sit down. I'd never done this before. Never had God *asked* me to do such a thing. It seemed a bit strange. But greater was my desire to be obedient.

As I kissed the foot of the first man, the Lord gave me a Word of knowledge about him, information only the man himself and God could know. I moved to the second man. Again there was a Word from the Lord. When I reached the third man, the Spirit moved in the same way as with the first two. But I heard God's voice again.

"Now you know where I was when I was here on earth. I became a servant. If you are to serve Me, this is where you must be for all men."

The impact of His words brought sudden understanding of the teaching Jesus gave when He washed the disciples' feet, as recorded in John 13:4-15. Here was Christ, the King, doing that relegated to servants or slaves and so misunderstood that even Peter didn't want to have a part in it. "Then wash all of me, Lord," he had pleaded.

As I continued on my mission around the room, men began breaking and weeping, each in turn realizing a new dimension of servanthood. Soon I was aware that the chapter's president, led to perform the same act, was following me. God's holiness and Presence charged the atmosphere.

Shortly before this, at an FGBMFI Men's Advance, the Lord had sent a brother to share with me that I must have a contrite spirit and broken heart; that I must always walk with a low profile. Although the Word came through a man, I knew it was God speaking.

I didn't know God was using my obedience to set the stage in my heart for another event, the one in India.

On that day in 1982, God placed with me Rev. Schack of Switzerland and Rev. Dallmann of Germany, brothers whom I greatly respected.

However, I had to admit a measure of concern when Rev. Shack began speaking about love, the subject to which I'd been led. But as he progressed, I realized he had a different approach than mine. Love was also Rev. Dallmann's subject, but again, it was different than either mine or Rev. Schack's. Their anointed messages created a beautiful air of expectancy.

Then it was my turn. After sharing for several minutes, I was prompted to relate the experience of the FGBMFI home meeting several years before — how God had shown me what it means to be a servant.

When next He directed me to kiss the feet of the young Indian, I saw Jesus' feet represented in those rough, swarthy ones beneath my lips.

I knew some of the thoughts and feelings coursing

through the broken, repentant young man I'd ministered to. I'd been the recipient of a similar act from Linda Toulson, Dick's wife, just prior to my first trip to India.

The congregation at home had gathered for prayer, with the laying on of hands, anointing me with oil for the work I'd been called to do. Love was expressed as we washed one another's feet.

After a few minutes of such fellowship, Linda stepped toward me. We watched as she allowed her beautiful reddish-blond hair to fall from its neat bun to its full length below her waist. Kneeling, she dipped her hands in the basin, washed my feet, then lovingly began drying them with some of her soft tresses. Tears flowed freely down my cheeks.

"Jesus, now I know how you must have felt when the woman did this for you," was my thought. And I knew the humility it demanded from Linda, since she prized her lovely hair.

I'd been the receiver of humble service. Now I was prepared to serve.

# Chapter Twenty

# Deliverance

*"[He] answered and said, Lord, I am not worthy that thou shouldest come under my roof: but speak the word only, and my servant shall be healed"* (Matt. 8:8).

A seventeen-year-old girl was critically ill in the Geneva, New York hospital. Friends of the family who lived some distance away called to ask if I'd go and pray for her. My tight schedule delayed my visit and there was another call. She was dying, the doctors unable to treat her since they couldn't diagnose the problem.

When I was finally able to visit the girl, I found she'd been transferred to a Rochester hospital, perhaps fifty miles away. I first felt guilt for not having gotten there sooner. But somehow I knew that my delay had been God-ordained.

As I stepped down the hall to leave, I began to pray.

"O God, how can I pray for this girl if I can't find her?" I questioned.

"You can pray for her right here, right now," I heard.

Immediately, I began to pray fervently, asking God to send His Spirit to effect the healing this girl desperately needed.

After returning home, I received a phone call informing me she'd been healed at the same time I'd prayed. The following day she was released and able to return to school.

"Speak the word only," the centurion had told Jesus. God's power was able to penetrate distance and obstacles. In these last days, God is calling us not to limit His power. We can't put Him into the small box of our thinking, confining Him to our realm. We must enter the spiritual Kingdom, appropriating the rights and privileges given us through Jesus Christ, our Lord.

Through His Name, we've been given power of attorney, as it were, and I believe God is pleased when we exercise that power by faith. Just as Jesus sent His power to heal a servant, so He sends power today to heal as we speak by faith.

It was at a small FGMFI meeting that we were told of a suicidal young man in a sanitorium. Demonic influence was mentioned. Dick Toulson offered to stand in proxy for the hospitalized man, and we all knelt to pray.

I began to speak in a strange tongue and had an unusual sense of God's power. As I reached out and touched Dick's beard, he fell over on the floor.

In a few days the report reached us. The day after we'd prayed, the young man jumped out of bed, all suicidal tendencies gone. Furthermore, he remained totally delivered from fears and other evils which had possessed him.

In another meeting, a woman spoke about her son who was acting strangely, involved in a cult many miles away. Again, a man agreed to stand in proxy. He went out in the Spirit as the group prayed together, casting out the demons by the power of God. I asked that the same Spirit moving through this man would go into the woman's son.

Although the man standing in proxy was gentle and mild-mannered, suddenly rage filled his face. In the

Name of Jesus. I commanded the spirits to leave while I held him by the wrists for two or three minutes. Violent demons fought and taunted in raucous voices. Soon the man was still. In a few moments he was able to tell us that the demons had left the young man for whom we were praying, but had entered into himself, desiring to destroy us.

Such ministry is not to be undertaken lightly. Much wisdom and guidance of the Holy Spirit is necessary in these situations. One should never attempt to deal with the enemy in another's life without that guidance. But God is all powerful, and we must remember that "...greater is He that is in [us] than he that is in the world" (I John 4:4).

\* \* \* \* \* \* \*

After God anointed me and I'd gone out in the Spirit for the first time, it seemed that whenever He wanted my attention, as soon as I'd raise my hands to pray I would fall under His anointing. Then He'd begin to speak.

On one such occasion, I was visiting in Jo Teske's home in Auburn. I'd perched myself on one of the kitchen stools; but as we prayed together, the Spirit of the Lord moved beautifully and I fell to the floor. It wasn't a hard fall. In fact, it seemed I was falling into a pillow.

"You will be casting out demons in My Name," Jesus declared.

The very next night June and I were in Auburn, where I'd just finished a time of teaching.

Suddenly a young nurse spoke up. "At times I seem to have confusion," she shared.

After assuring her that God is not the author of confusion, we began to pray. As she stood, I laid my hands on her head. Prior to this, I didn't even know confusion could be a spirit. But with the leading of the Holy Spirit, I commanded confusion to leave. She fell over under the anointing and I spoke again to confusion. With that, the young woman became violent.

"In the Name of Jesus, confusion come out!" I commanded again. A strange voice answered me through her mouth: "You can't do that to me," it said.

"Jesus Christ can," I retorted. "Now be gone immediately!"

There was a shrill scream.

"All of you come out," I continued, not knowing until that moment that more than one evil spirit was present.

Now a hideous laugh mocked me, followed by more screams and wretching. Once again I commanded with authority in the Name of Jesus. Calm replaced the writhing. The young woman's hands shot into the air and praises to God began flowing from her mouth.

Following these initial experiences against demons, there were many more, each different. But I learned to rely upon the Holy Spirit for direction and wisdom.

I also learned that there is no specific pattern or prescription for deliverance. When spiritual powers are involved they will manifest themselves in a variety of ways, attempting to intimidate, scare, deceive, and finally destroy. Often a spirit will say, "I'm gone," "I'm not here," or "I'm all right." Screams sometimes accompany a manifestation.

****

"No, I don't want prayer," the woman shouted.

Esther, one of the church women, had brought her friend, Jane, to me for prayer. "She might need deliverance," Esther warned. Jane had been a cult member.

As we'd begun to talk, I suddenly knew that talking wouldn't help. The Lord told me that Jane was definitely demon-possessed. When I'd mentioned prayer, she'd yelled.

"Come out in the Name of Jesus," I now commanded.

Jane fell to the floor, screaming. Each time I spoke Jesus' Name, she'd thrash and scream, knocking over chairs and a lamp in the process. But we knew the demonic forces were leaving.

Esther positioned herself on top of her friend to suppress the demonic display.

"Everything is all right now. I'm okay," we heard a weirdly sweet voice say during one of Jane's quiet moments.

"Speak My Name," the Lord instructed. As I did, violence returned.

Suddenly Jane began to levitate with Esther still on her back. In a prone position, she was suspended in the air and reached for the doorknob. Esther and I had never seen anything quite like this before.

"In the Name of Jesus Christ," I spoke, and down Jane and Esther crashed to the floor. Finally, the last demon was gone and Jane, now smiling and free, wanted prayer.

Today, she remains free, loving the Lord.

**** 

As word got around that many people had been delivered from demonic forces, phone calls began coming.

I stopped at Jo's home another day before going into the prison and received a call while there. The young man on the other end informed me that his friend, Shirley, earlier had been locked in a padded cell of a psychiatric ward. She'd been meeting with a woman who declared herself to be a witch. The witch had read a Greek chant to Shirley, and at that moment, something strange had happened. A power had invaded the girl along with a feeling of something possessing her. Even her features changed.

He went on to tell me that a girlfriend of Shirley's had visited her. As they talked, Shirley's normal expression suddenly faded and was replaced by a weird, diabolical look. Shirley, of slight build, had lunged toward her heavy-set friend, grabbed her, and threw the girl against the wall. Horrified, her friend ran from the house.

When a priest Shirley called agreed to visit her and bless her apartment, the girl rushed on him, ripping open one side of his face with her fingernails.

The fellow even described how Shirley's neck muscles would swell out sideways, cobra-fashion.

He'd heard of other deliverances and asked if I could help.

"If you can have her here at the house, I'll pray for her when I'm finished with the prison ministry," I assured the troubled young man. He said he'd try to get her there, although even two strong men had admitted having problems trying to physically control her.

When I returned, I learned that Shirley's friends had her on the back porch. Nervously they sat around her, thinking she might try to run.

I quickly excused myself and headed for the bathroom to pray.

"Give me guidance, Lord," I implored. "Let your Holy Spirit flow through me now in Jesus' Name."

My leading was to sit beside her and just visit for a few minutes. So I did. As we talked, I reached out, taking hold of one wrist. For twenty minutes our conversation continued, and I noted an increasing calm settling over Shirley's troubled features.

"How are you feeling now?" I asked.

"Better than I have in days," was her reply. "But look at my wrist." Where I'd held it, there was swelling three times its normal size.

"There's been resistance, but that's all right," I answered. "The Holy Spirit's been working in you and the swelling will go. Are you ready to go in and have us pray with you for full deliverance?"

"Yes," was her definite answer.

With the Holy Spirit having prepared the way,

deliverance came quickly. As Shirley went to her knees, she went out in the Spirit. In only two or three minutes the demons came out, screaming a bit as they left. Shirley was then totally free and began praising Jesus. Several years later she called me, telling of her continuing close walk with the Lord.

We can know all the right words, even be professional clergymen. But the power of God's Holy Spirit is the answer.

Had someone merely told me of such happenings, I doubt I'd have believed them. But with direct exposure came a new certainty in the truth of the Word. The Bible became even more alive.

It was at a church that I met a young man who asked if he could bring a friend for deliverance. The friend was being tormented by spirits of hatred and murder. When two others had prayed for him he'd become so angry he pounded a garbage can, compressing it to the ground with his hands.

"I want deliverance, but I'm afraid I might hurt you," he said upon entering our home. I assured him he wouldn't. Then three young fellows and I began to pray. In a few moments the young man fell under the anointing, after which he started hissing, barking and snarling. Suddenly his neck swelled out like a Cobra's, just as I'd heard about Shirley. Striking at us, he grabbed one of my arms with a vise-like grip. I commanded him in the Name of Jesus to release me, and in a few minutes he was completely delivered from all demons. Later he married and now is leading a successful Christian life.

One of the young men told afterward of seeing Michael, the Archangel, hovering as we ministered.

How wonderful to know that the same forces at work in Daniel's time are not relegated to the pages of the Bible! God has made all the powers of the Kingdom available to us — and it isn't our battle at all, but the Lord's. Although we may not feel our significance when we line ourselves up beside those in the Word of God, we must see that God is willing to go to the least of those serving Him, just as He did with Daniel, Gideon or any others.

This particular young man we prayed with was a Christian, but he had been careless in his living, keeping steady company with non-Christians. And he wasn't regularly in the Word or in fellowship. So he'd opened the door for the enemy. We counseled him after praying, pointing out his need to take the authority given him in the Name of Jesus and to deal with the enemy himself.

How easy it is to run to another every time there's a problem or deliverance is needed! Getting into God's Word is a must, for it's a sword against the enemy. We must also put on the full armor as described in Ephesians chapter 6, realizing that our fight isn't against flesh and blood. Then we can resist Satan's fiery darts and stand victoriously.

While in the Auburn Christian Bookstore one day, I heard about Glenn. When a teenager, he had made a deal with Satan — if Satan would give him the gift of music, he'd give Satan his soul. Now, at age twenty-four, Glenn had just been released from a mental institution, his brain badly burned from LSD. Friends hoped I'd meet him.

"You'll be doing battle face-to-face with satan," I heard in my spirit some days later during a time of prayer. So I wasn't surprised when Glenn and I met in the bookstore the following day.

Filthy, torn clothes hung limply from his thin body. I glimpsed traces of handsome features and a once well-built physique beneath the dirt and rags. His hands twitched constantly and his deep-set eyes peered furtively in all directions. Suspicious and apprehensive, Glenn trusted no one, not even himself. His home was the street.

"You don't know what it's like to sell your soul and

then be controlled by this evil," he said. "Satan tells me everything I have to do. I can't stand the torment."

We talked on while I held Glenn's hands. A peace and quiet settled around the two of us as we stood visiting. He wanted to walk with God, he said, but something inside prevented him.

"There's always that voice. I keep hearing that voice," he spoke haltingly. "And any time I have a good thought, something tells me to stop thinking that way."

"Would you let me pray with you?" I asked.

"Yes," Glenn blurted out. But suddenly, a different voice expressing itself through his mouth said, "No, don't do this."

"I've got to."

"No, you can't," the voice countered.

Confusion filled the air around us. Never had I seen such a vivid battle between good and evil.

"Let's remove our shoes, because God is going to be present," I was inspired to suggest.

Three other people joined us as we knelt. While they prayed, I began commanding the demonic forces to leave. When I touched Glenn's head, he fell on his face under God's power. But as soon as he touched the floor, another power picked him up, setting him back on his knees before me. Beads of sweat glistened on his forehead as one voice spoke, then another.

"What do you think of this Scripture?" he asked.

"Don't get into that with him," God instructed me.

"This isn't the time to talk Scripture," I answered. Then I commanded again. "Come out in the Name of Jesus."

Fright filled Glenn's eyes as his body jerked back and forth.

"Satan, what do I say? What do I say? What do I do?" a voice pleaded as Glenn fell over, then was lifted up again. I saw panic and knew the demons were losing control.

"In the Name of Jesus Christ I take authority and bind the spirits," I spoke firmly.

"You can't do that," a voice hollered, and with that, Glenn jumped to his feet, grabbed his shoes and fled, shirt-tail flying behind him.

"Go after him," the others instructed.

"God will go after him," I shared insightfully. "Let's pray." My prayer was greatly strengthened by the Holy Spirit's anointing.

Some days later, Glenn attended a meeting nearby where another minister and I prayed for him again. During our prayer session, for the first time I smelled the putrid odor of Satan.

"What is your name?" I felt to ask.

Through another individual came the words, "I am the keeper of the abyss."

I don't remember just how long it was when I next saw Glenn, but when I did, what a surprise awaited me. He was clean, neatly dressed, and had gotten a job and apartment. His mind was clear and he was free of the opposing evil forces which had sought to destroy him.

In a neat letter to me in a few days, Glenn expressed his thanks for the ministry and for his freedom.

During another visit in Auburn a short time later, I inquired about Glenn. The answer saddened me. While crossing a river, he'd fallen from the bridge and drowned.

I didn't understand his death, but I knew God had set Glenn free. I had an assurance that he'd gone to be with the Lord.

# Chapter Twenty-one

# Translated

*"And when they were come up out of the water, the Spirit of the Lord caught away Philip, that the eunuch saw him no more: and he went on his way rejoicing. But Philip was found at Azotus: and passing through he preached in all the cities, till he came to Caesarea"* (Acts 8:39, 40.)

Nothing about this day had been normal. We'd arrived in Syracuse the night before to be at the hospital at six a.m. Our friend, Captain Charlie Whitacre of the Salvation Army, was to have surgery that morning and wanted us to pray with him beforehand.

Charlie had had a heart condition for several years, suffering nine heart attacks. The doctors planned to replace two valves and perform by-pass surgery. But as we prayed together, God told me Charlie wouldn't need the scheduled repair work, that He had healed him.

So we waited for the good news. Soon a surgeon appeared, announcing that new valves weren't needed. They were just fine. He described it as amazing. The doctors, however, had performed one by-pass.

So we were in a joyous mood, although tired from a lack of sleep and the hospital wait.

It was as we worked our way across Syracuse to our hotel that a strange event happened. It was sudden, as if June and I were part of a movie. One moment we were driving down a familiar residential street, and the next we were on a four-lane highway. A three-thousand-pound car somehow had been "catapulted" by God's Spirit.

"We've just been translated!" I exclaimed to June.

"Why?" was her reasonable question as she continued the knitting project in her lap. I loved her practicality.

"I don't know. Maybe it's just to get us to the hotel sooner," I responded. "But I have no idea where we are."

Then I recognized our hotel just ahead.

In retrospect, I believe God permits such significant experiences for various reasons. He wants to show His power, His ability, and prove that His Word is true.

In reading the story of Enoch, who was suddenly snatched away to be with God, we understand it to mean he was translated. Elijah was swept off the earth by a fiery chariot as Elisha watched. Although these recountings are in the Old Testament, in the New Testament, the Book of Acts tells that Philip was caught up by the Spirit and immediately placed in Azotus, a suburb of his hometown of Caesarea, after he had baptized the eunuch.

When Jesus was resurrected, He appeared in the midst of His disciples. Although He was in His glorified body, it's an illustration of what God can do.

I've read and heard others tell of similar experiences — the late David DuPlessis, a great man of God, was picked up by the Spirit and placed on the doorstep of someone needing immediate help; a missionary was taken across a river to protect him from the chasing tribes.

Hebrews 13:8 reminds us that Jesus Christ is the same yesterday, today and forever. Those who believe His Word and place no limits on Him will see His power manifested, His Word made alive. I believe He grants such experiences to remind us that He hasn't changed.

I believe these are also for building our faith. In seemingly impossible situations, we can remember what God has done in the past and our faith is renewed. How often He would remind us, "Didn't I multiply the loaves and fishes? Didn't Jesus walk on water? Why are you hesitating?"

Scientists have accomplished remarkable things. Researchers and clinical scientists have performed miracles in medicine. Our aerospace programs have brought many improvements, even in commercial traffic. We're tremendously grateful for all of these.

But we must remember that Almighty God performs the unexplainable, overwhelming miracles beyond the greatest of man's abilities. We must not lean to our own understanding, but "trust in the Lord with all [our] heart" (Prov. 3:5, 6).

The human body is a daily reminder of God's greatness. In Psalm 139:14 we read that we are fearfully and wonderfully made. As we reflect on the intricacies of the eye alone — its ability to focus, distinguish color, coordinate movement — we see the awesomeness of our Creator. No doctor can explain this marvelous creation.

The universe, with its billions of stars light-years away, forces us to admit the Intelligence behind it all. The Bible states that God put the innumerable stars in the heavens and knows each by name.

As I look at a translation experience from this perspective, I see it as a minor miracle that God is able to perform.

# Chapter Twenty-two

# God's Body Shop

*"The Lord is on my side; I will not fear: what can man do unto me?"* (Ps. 118:6)

I heard the sickening crunch of metal as a car rushed through the intersection and into the left side of my car. We tipped up slightly onto the right wheels, then rocked to a standstill.

My first thoughts were rather unchristian ones as I considered the car's caved-in side. We were in the middle of five o'clock traffic in Syracuse, and I quickly thought of all the hassle of notifying the police, making out reports, then later waiting for estimates and repairs to be made.

A friend, John, had wanted to spend some time with me, and so was along for the ride. Fortunately, neither of us was hurt.

As I pushed the car door open, I saw an older lady sitting in a white car. Suddenly, compassion flooded me as I thought of how she must feel over what she'd just done. God's power welled up on the inside, causing me to do something unusual.

"I'm a Christian and I love God," I spoke, as I stuck

my head in her left window. Amazement registered on her face.

"Oh, I'm a Catholic," she said quickly.

"Praise the Lord," I replied. "Are you a Christian?"

She studied me for a moment.

"Yes, I am."

"Then we won't have a problem." I smiled, and relief replaced her look of concern.

By this time John had joined me, and together we helped her from her car.

Anxious to survey the damages, we hurried to the side of my Olds Cutlass. I stared in disbelief. There was no dent, no scratch, not even a speck of dust out of place. The woman knew she'd smashed the left rear door.

"I don't understand. I don't understand," she kept repeating, while she walked back and forth, trying to find some hint of damage.

"God has done something here," I said, as I gently placed my hands on her shoulders and stopped her pacing.

"It says in Proverbs 3:5, 'Lean not on your own understanding, but trust in God.' I don't understand how God can put a car back together, but He's able, and for some reason He did."

Then we turned to study the damage to her car. The brown paint from mine was ground into the metal, as well as into the white paint on the right front end and fender of her Chevy. Several small dents filled the areas. John and I measured the height of the paint smears, then measured all along the side of the Olds. Still we could find no mark. We knew God had performed a miracle.

"I...don't...believe..." John said slowly while shaking his head. "But knowing you, I'd believe anything!" He'd been present to see dramatic healings and had heard of the wonderful things God had done in our lives.

He had been a body-man, so he spent several

minutes explaining how she could remove my paint from her metal at little expense.

As we waved and drove away, she stood in front of her car. "I don't understand," she still repeated. "I don't understand."

There are many who call themselves believers and are involved in churches, but don't trust in the Lord, trying to figure out everything with their own understanding. The Word states that God's ways are not man's ways, and the only way we can understand at all is spiritually. Jesus said, "God is a Spirit: and they that worship Him must worship Him in spirit and in truth" (John 4:24).

As John and I drove away from the accident scene, we both knew that something very special had happened. However, there was also the sense that more was ahead. Little did I know that God was preparing this young man's heart to receive the baptism of the Holy Spirit.

We stopped in Auburn to visit Jo Teske, and Jo shared with John about the baptism. I'd already prayed, "Lord, if this is the day for him to receive the baptism, You prepare his heart."

Soon he was ready for prayer. Immediately he began to sing in a heavenly language. This was a new spiritual dimension for him, and the beginning of much more. God had used the day's events to show John Himself, His love and His power.

\* \* \*

"...With men this is impossible; but with God all things are possible" (Matt. 19:26).

A handful of people filled the small living room in an Auburn home. Dude was one of them.

"Does anybody need prayer?" I asked.

"Dude, get prayer," a friend kindly commanded this visiting lady from New England.

"I don't know if I can have you pray for this," the visitor countered, red-faced with embarrassment.

"What's the matter?" I asked curiously.

"I've been missing three vertebrae in my back since birth," she answered. "And I've had to wear a back brace all my life."

"I'll ask you two questions. Then tell me if you want me to pray for you or not." I studied her puzzled face for a moment, then continued.

"Did God create you?"

"Yes," she hastily replied.

"Can Jesus Christ do anything He wants to do?"

"Yes," she answered again, then added, "All right, pray for me."

I didn't hesitate, anxious to see what God would do for this lovely lady. Quickly, I stretched my hands toward her, but just as I started to say, "In the Name of Jesus," something unusual happened. Sparks flew from my fingers directly into her head. My daughter standing behind felt their impact. Dude fell back in the chair under the Spirit's anointing. The sudden display of God's power startled all of us.

By stretching the imagination, one might have concluded that the sparks were merely static electricity. However, the results left no doubt. I'd known only of the problem in Dude's back, but had been led to pray, "Lord, heal her whole body." When I heard the report, I knew why.

Not only did healthy vertebrae fill the once-empty space in her back, but a growth had fallen off her back, as well. And God had healed her of glaucoma. Six months later, there was still no trace of the disease.

Dude threw away the brace she no longer needed.

# Chapter Twenty-three

# Chicken Coop Chapel

*"Fear not, little flock; for it is your Father's good pleasure to give you the kingdom"* (Luke 12:32).

The floor of the "upper room" shook and a lamp at the end of the room rocked precariously on the stand beneath as thirty-five people sang exuberantly before the Lord.

Our daughter, Mary Louise, and Dick Toulson had begun a Bible study in our living room with seven or eight people. As it grew, we had to move to this larger room.

It was 1977, soon after the Lord had led me here and called me into a new walk with a greater anointing.

Many wonderful things were happening in the Bible study — people were making commitments to Jesus Christ, being baptized in the Holy Ghost and healed. And we were growing spiritually as we studied the Word together.

Now I had the impression that we were to turn the old chicken coop on the back of our property into a place of worship. The idea seemed absurd, but I couldn't deny the tug in my spirit.

I knelt on a bale of the mildewed, unsalable hay in the old building.

"God, if You want this place, You'll have to sell the hay," I spoke, knowing this would be a good test of my inner direction.

The next day my neighbor stopped, asking if he could buy it.

"It's old," I warned him.

"I don't care. I want it anyway," he said quickly.

Soon he was back, cleaning out the chicken coop.

Next, with Luke 14:28 fresh in mind, I computed on yellow ledger paper what I thought the transformation would cost. Five thousand dollars was the total.

Later that week a Christian sister from Auburn saw me.

"The Lord has told me I must give you five thousand dollars," she said.

I'd told no one of the amount I had in mind. But I didn't want to accept her gift, knowing she wasn't a rich person. We agreed to pray.

"Accept the money. I will bless her for giving it," I heard the Lord say while I prayed in my Rochester office the next week.

So work began on the Chicken Coop Chapel. Both men and women came evenings and weekends, toting saws, hammers, and nails. Old ceiling joists, doors and windows were torn out and replaced with new. The chicken coop began to take on a different look.

One brother and I worked together several evenings to reinforce the ceiling. To accomplish this, we had to cut cross pieces, run them from rafter to rafter, then attach plywood plates to give added strength. After repeated attempts to drive the nails in without their bending, almost in desperation, I spoke, "In the Name of Jesus,"and the nail went in effortlessly. I continued to speak the Name of Jesus over each nail, and into the wood they went with no more problems.

Meanwhile, my friend Bill was pounding and bending nails, one after another.

"How are you doing that?" he finally asked.

"Just speak the Name of Jesus and give Him the glory," I instructed. He tried it, and sure enough, the nails began going in straight. We praised and worshiped the Lord as we easily drove about twenty-five pounds of nails into the ceiling.

A retiree, Leon Van Norman, worked many days. For warmth as we worked or for meetings during the cold weather, he built a woodstove out of two barrels.

A large project he tackled involved removing a door and replacing it with a picture window. After several days, he was ready on Saturday for help with the installation. Five men lifted it, but quickly discovered that somehow Leon had miscalculated. The opening was too small. We tried forcing and prying it into place with no success. The window was a full quarter-inch too large on the sides. After lowering it, we studied the problem. Neither enlarging the opening nor cutting down the window would be a small task.

"Men, I believe the Lord wants us to pray about this before we do anything," I suddenly said. So we bowed our heads and asked the Lord to cause the window to fit without any further carpentry work. None seemed surprised when we lifted the window and pushed it into the opening, needing not one tool to complete the job. It fit perfectly. How we praised the Lord for showing us His power!

The outside of the chicken coop was covered with ugly tar paper. We wanted good siding, but funds were low. I knelt and prayed.

"Lord, we need siding for this building. We can't provide it, so I'm asking You to do it."

The next day a man stopped at the chapel.

"Do you need siding?" he questioned.

"Yes, as a matter of fact we do," I replied.

"How much do you need?"

"Six squares."

"Isn't that interesting?" he said. "I have six squares of cedar siding in my garage. It's been there for fifteen years, left over from a job I had done, and is still in the original packaging. You can have it."

God was indeed our Provider.

We began holding our meetings in the chicken coop, the concrete floor allowing us a freedom we'd not had in the upper room. Sometimes it was a bit cold and drafty, and we didn't have toilet facilities yet. But we didn't mind the inconveniences. God was moving in a wonderful way.

On Easter, 1978, nearly thirty people met for a sunrise service and breakfast. Only the east end of the chapel was usable where we'd placed a scrap of carpeting and a large table. Although most had to leave to attend their churches, twelve of us remained to share communion.

As I turned to pick up the sacraments, I was aware of the Presence of Jesus at the table. Our consciousness of Him heightened and I began to pray while some of us fell to the floor under the power of His Holy Spirit. Warmth and joy flooded us. As we began to worship the Lord, feeling His presence in our midst, there was a great sense of unity. We were certain God had put His blessing on this little place. We knew this was just the beginning of many great things.

God told me that the chapel was to open as a church on January 7, 1979, although I was pastoring the new work in Auburn which God was also blessing.

Concern gripped us as we neared the end of the year with many tasks still undone. But everyone cooperated again. Bathrooms were finished, walls painted, lights installed, and even part of the kitchen was done. Men and women had set aside other pursuits and given of themselves.

Our next need was for carpeting. We wanted to carpet the chapel, which was 26 x 40 feet, the room next to it for the children, and a small study. As usual, we gathered and prayed.

It was only a few days before Christmas, and as we shopped for the right carpeting we found that to get what we needed involved considerable expense and delay.

Finally we stopped at a store whose specialty wasn't carpeting. But a salesman directed us to follow him to the back, where he pointed to a carpet the exact color and quality we had in mind.

"It's interesting that the name of this carpet is 'Revelation,' " he commented.

We knew this was what we had to have, but he explained the impossibility of delivery before January 7. With Christmas approaching, the carpet having to be shipped from Georgia, and normal delivery taking at least two weeks, there was no way it could be accomplished. He even suggested the possibility that stock was depleted and the carpet would have to be manufactured.

"We prayed about this and are trusting God to provide it," I said. "So please call and we'll go from there. We're just going to believe."

As several of us worked in the chapel later that day, the salesman called. He had contacted the plant in Georgia, and two pieces, just the right size, were in stock. There was only one problem: because of different runs, there could be a variation in color. Did we want them anyway?

Quickly we prayed together.

"Order them," the Lord instructed.

Three days later there was another phone call from the salesman. "We don't understand this," he stated, "But the carpeting is in." A Christian brother of another church, a professional carpet layer, helped install it. Even the names of the padding, "New Steps," the color, "Harvest Time," and the manufacturer,

"Horizon," held special significance for us. They seemed to indicate God's blessing and direction.

On January 7, 1979, twenty-some people gathered at ten a.m. to worship the Lord. We'd chosen the name of United Fellowship Chapel to express the unity which existed in our small body.

With severe northwesterly winds in upstate New York, we quickly saw the need to add a small porch as a windbreak. But the project had been delayed several times. Finally, one day in 1981 several men gathered to start a foundation for it.

As we prayed beforehand, the Lord told me that we needed more than a windbreak. We needed an additional room for the growing congregation of nearly sixty. The men present agreed, each having sensed the same directive. We decided to pray further. Certain men were assigned the task of drawing plans.

Those they submitted called for a 24 x 40 foot room with a basement beneath. Money was scarce, so we built as funds were available. Again, both men and women donated their time, mixing mortar, lifting block and pounding nails. The flock drew together, and we watched the building take further form.

With one member using his huge Trojan earth-mover and a local tractor company allowing me the use of a back hoe, we dug a foundation. A group called the "Star of David Singers" had performed at the church the night before. Now they helped put in footers and build forms.

Soon the concrete company arrived and concrete began filling the wheelbarrows. One man after another dumped concrete into the hole while others tamped it and still others rough-troweled the mix. Nearly twenty feet of wall remained to be done when one elder announced that the concrete was running out. The driver would have to get more.

Suddenly the power and Presence of the Lord filled me.

"The driver's not going back to get more concrete. God is going to multiply it," I shouted. "You don't even have to stop working. Just agree with me as we pray."

I asked God, in the Name of Jesus, to multiply the concrete, then instructed the driver to turn the machine on again. The slide was once more aimed at a wheelbarrow. Suddenly concrete was pouring down the chute. This mix, with a pinkish tint, was a bit darker and heavier, however, than the previous mix. We rejoiced and praised the Lord as each man took a turn filling his wheelbarrow, about twenty-seven loads in all, to fill the remainder of the wall.

"I still have concrete left!" the driver informed us when the wall was completed. I thought of the back entrance. Quickly we constructed another form. With the help of the back hoe and with the forms in place, more dark gray cement began pouring out.

Soon the slab was completed, but still more concrete was left. We praised the Lord and built another form for an entrance on the opposite end of the chapel. The mix pushed its way down the chute until that slab was finished. Now not a drop was left. Upon measuring, we found we'd used over nine cubic yards of cement from a truck that held only seven.

An inscription was needed. The leader of the Star of David Singers agreed to "sign" the miracle God had performed. Pressing an index finger into the smooth cement, she wrote her name, "Shushe," which means "Rose of Sharon," added, "In Jesus' Name," in Hebrew, the Star of David symbol, and finally the date. The job now seemed complete.

Next we wondered if we'd get the top section on before winter. But money kept flowing and so many volunteers worked that when snow came, the roof, walls, windows and doors were in place.

The next year we knew it was time to consider permanent siding for the addition. After prayer we decided that uncut stones from the surrounding fields would be just right. Two men in the fellowship were already proficient in stone-laying, and they taught the other workers. Little by little over the summer, stones were added to the structure. The building soon took on quite a professional look and we stood back, amazed at what God had achieved through us.

# Chapter Twenty-four

# The Threaded Holes

*"Call unto me, and I will answer thee, and shew thee great and mighty things, which thou knowest not"* (Jer. 33:3).

Our Canandaigua "farm" sported seventy-seven acres, forty-five of which were tillable. Not wanting to see land lay idle, I purchased some equipment. Before our son Jim came to help, I handled all the spring planting of our corn and repaired the tractors. The latter wasn't my forte but, when necessary, I could do a reasonably good job.

We'd had problems with the brakes on the tractor I'd purchased and they needed to be replaced. Upon taking one of them apart, I discovered a leaking seal. The repair job required the removal of a ten-inch round plate. At the local dealership, I learned this would be a very difficult task. One of the men suggested I try using a tool they'd made that might help with the job.

I confidently crawled under the tractor, tool in hand, and issued up a prayer. "God," I implored, "Please help me get this plate off."

It was seven in the evening when I began, and for

three hours I struggled to remove the plate, oil dripping on my face and aching arms. But it wouldn't budge.

"If only there were a couple of threaded holes in that plate, one on each side," I thought, "I could just put bolts in there and pull the plate right off." It seemed so simple a solution. Later models had such a convenience, I knew.

At ten o'clock I gave up, almost in utter disgust. It had seemed like such a waste of time.

As I trudged into the house to clean up, I cried out to the Lord. "God, I asked You to help me."

Suddenly I stopped and began laughing, knowing I couldn't waver, knowing that God is faithful. He'd done so many things for me.

"Ah, I know now, God. When I come out in the morning You're going to show me exactly how to repair that tractor. Praise the Lord!" I continued my rejoicing as I scrubbed the grease from my face and hands and headed for bed.

Early the next morning I excitedly crawled under the tractor again. My heart was already prepared by my prayer time, for I'd asked God for this day to go well — that I'd accomplish what I'd purposed to do.

I could scarcely believe what I saw! There on one side, bright and shiny, was a freshly-drilled hole in the plate, complete with new threads. It shone in contrast to the darkened plate. Quickly checking the opposite side, I found a matching hole. I ran to my tool box and there, to my amazement, were two odd-looking bolts with square heads.

"It's got to be — God's answered my prayer!" I concluded.

Anxious to try the bolts, I hurried back to the tractor and easily screwed them into the new holes. In less than two minutes I had the plate off and in my hands.

When June came out a while later to check on my work, I pushed the plate in front of her.

"Do you see anything unusual?" I asked.

"No, not other than the two freshly-threaded holes."

I then shared with her what God had done.

In the natural, it was totally impossible to accept. But in the Spirit, it was completely in concert with God's ability, love and desire to answer the prayers of His servants. In my own mind I couldn't find any way to understand how God could do such a thing as this. Because it was such a hard-to-reach place, even with the best power tool this job would have been impossible.

God had performed another miracle.

\* \* \* \* \* \* \*

"Jack, I don't understand this," my salesman friend began. "I was driving half an hour ago and the Lord told me to come to your house immediately. So here I am. What is it?"

I told him how I'd climbed about twenty feet up an electrical pole to disconnect overhead wires and connect underground wires to the barn behind the house. However, I hadn't known that the pole had rotted under the ground's surface. I'd heard the creaking and felt the breaking. The descent seemed like an eternity.

My thoughts had been of how the pole could crush me, or of how I could easily be entangled in the wires. The four-foot steel clothes pole, connected to this pole, had impaled itself into the ground, just inches from my body. Although I landed free, all my weight had been on one foot. It was twisted awkwardly and felt broken. Pains shot up my leg. As I laid hands on the ankle and foot, I began to pray.

"Lord, I need another man to help me," I added to my prayer for healing. Just after that my friend pulled into the drive. Now I described the help I needed. Together we dug a trench to bury the wires. While digging, I noted that all the pain was gone. My foot was healed.

Next, I had to make a trip to the city. With the wires

buried and my foot fine, I had other business to tend to. As I started out, I was reminded of the events of the night before.

I'd arrived home about two a.m. from my usual day of ministry at Auburn Prison. Immediately June met me, excitedly telling me about how our daughter, Mary Louise, along with a neighbor girl, were down the road caring for some horses. June said something about an accident, and with that, I was back in the car, ready to help.

I'd found the girls holding three horses. As I inspected them by flashlight, they seemed okay. But the fourth horse was a pathetic sight, hardly able to stand, with one side terribly distended. There was obvious damage to the hind quarters also, and the hips looked broken. They stood together, horses and girls, looking forlorn in the darkness. No one had come to claim the animals. It was as if they'd suddenly appeared.

The deputy sheriff soon arrived, debating whether to shoot the injured animal or not. Trying to get it to walk was fruitless, as it nearly collapsed.

When I arrived, I'd prayed, "Lord, do something with this horse." I didn't know what else to do.

It seemed right to take the good horses to our paddock to stay overnight until the owner could be found. The remaining pitiful horse stood alone in the dark.

Now it was the following day, and as I approached I saw the animal was still standing, tied to a pole. I stopped and glanced around to see if anyone was nearby. Only a farmer plowed in a far field.

"In the Name of Jesus Christ, be healed," I commanded as I laid my hands on the horse. Then I drove on.

The next day I set out to see a neighbor. I intended to ask him if he knew where I might find a pole. He began telling of a horse he'd picked up from down the road.

Knowing the owner, he'd returned the horse, using his own trailer.

"How did you load that horse?" I asked, and described the injuries it had suffered.

"There was nothing wrong with it," he replied, dumbfounded. I told him of the $700 worth of damage to the car that struck the animal and also of my prayer for it.

I wasn't surprised at what God had done. I'd seen Him heal animals before. There was the time that Burt Nussey, the prison chaplain, and I had found a German shepherd lying against my car door. It got up, but could only walk on three legs. The fourth was badly twisted, and the poor dog held it close to his body.

"Call him back," the Lord commanded.

As the dog turned around, I spoke, "In the Name of Jesus, be healed." The leg untwisted and the dog walked away normally. Burt was so tickled he jumped up and down. In his newly characteristic manner, he filled the air with high-pitched hoots to express his joy in the Lord.

If God cares about animals, I thought, how much more He loves and cares for His children.

\* \* \* \*

It was late summer, and our family had driven to a park on Canandaigua Lake to picnic and enjoy some of the last good weather.

The seagulls gathered around the table, grabbing the corn puffs we tossed.

Suddenly we spied a gull with a fishing plug hanging from its beak.

"Lord, remove that plug from this bird in Jesus' Name," I prayed, feeling sorry for the helpless gull. But with a flap of its wings, out it flew, way over the lake.

"Lord, I really would have liked to have seen how You remove that plug from the bird so we'd know

You've heard and answered. We'd like to see it free," I quietly prayed.

Preparing to leave, we cleaned up the remaining corn puffs. Just then the injured bird landed beside us, plug still hanging from its mouth. The other birds hadn't responded to my coaxing. But now, as I dropped a corn puff beside me, this one toddled over. I reached down, quickly grabbing the bird around his wings.

Fortunately Jim, who'd driven his VW, had a trunk full of tools. He pulled out wire cutters and in a moment cut the plug.

We were thankful, again, to see God's care, even for a seagull.

# Chapter Twenty-five

# Vacation

*"Delight thyself also in the Lord; and he shall give thee the desires of thine heart"* (Ps. 37:4).

It had been a long time since June and I had had a vacation, and as I pondered the possibility of a trip, New Hampshire came to mind. We'd liked New England when we had visited the area before.

This fall day I prayed on my way to a dental appointment, asking God to work out a vacation.

Usually the dentist was all ready for me, but today the receptionist said I'd have a few minutes' wait. As I took a chair, I curiously noted a book on New England on the nearby stand. I opened it to an advertisement for a New Hampshire ski lodge near Mt. Washington, a spot we'd wanted to visit. The rate, which included some meals, was perfect for our pocketbook. I called the 800-number to make reservations when I got home.

Our request, "Lord, let us find accommodations for no more than twenty dollars per day as we travel," seemed rather unreasonable, considering the season.

The first night we decided to find a motel near Bennington, Vermont. But "no vacancy" signs met our searching eyes at each motel we passed. Finally we found a place with one room left. We'd take it, I told the desk clerk, although it was twenty-four dollars.

I called a dear Christian friend in a Vermont town some miles away. He suggested we meet him and his wife at church for Sunday service the next morning. So we did. Over lunch at their home we informed our friends of our vacation plans, but added we'd like to find a place to spend two more nights. Could they suggest somewhere for us to stay that night and Monday, we asked?

It was no problem, they assured us. They owned two cabins near Jackson, where we were headed. Neither was in use. I tucked their hand-drawn map into my shirt pocket. Then we waved good-bye and set off for the mountains.

Finally, after a careful search, we spied the narrow dirt road and wound our way back into the remote pine forest to the small rustic cabins. It was a quiet setting, well-suited to our tastes. We chose the larger cabin, although both were completely furnished. The peaceful night's rest was just what we needed before moving on to the ski lodge.

June and I had each been led to go on a partial fast, eating only the meals provided in the package. It proved to prepare us for sharing the Gospel with two Jewish couples. It was also a great opportunity to read and pray.

Back to the cabins we traveled after the two-day stay at the lodge. This time, though, we chose the smaller of the dark brown buildings. With no electricity, the oil lamps, our only light, shed a soft, cozy glow in the one-room cabin. We nestled in to enjoy more stillness.

Our friends had offered us a cabin for the week. But because of a commitment I'd made to speak at a Full Gospel Businessmen's breakfast on Saturday morning, I knew we'd have to begin working our way toward New York at the end of the week.

We reminded God of our desire to pay no more than

twenty dollars for a room and in Vermont found one
for that exact price.

On our final evening in New England, we again
looked for just the right spot. It was near six p.m., and
one motel after another had no room. Finally we
spotted an attractive, colonial-looking structure
amongst a grove of pines. Its only sign said "AAA."

"Did the Spirit quicken that place to you as we went
by?" June asked.

He had, so immediately I turned around and pulled
up to the office. Quickly I sized up the neat-looking
place, but curiously noted there wasn't one car out
front. I pushed open the office/living room door and a
hunched-over old woman, Hungarian, I learned, met
me.

"Sorry, no room. We're filled," she said brusquely.

I gaped in amazement. "Where are all the cars if
you're filled?" I quizzed.

"They've all gone to dinner."

A man stuck his head in the door as I still stood there.
Her answer to him was the same. Although I didn't
believe her, we had no choice but to drive on.

As I backed out, telling June of the woman and her
"full" motel, the Spirit of the Lord spoke.

"Stop and go back in. Pray for her healing."

I informed June of His instruction and hopped out,
leaving the car running, door open and June reading
her Bible. I assured her I'd return in a moment.

"Help me on this one, Lord," I implored, as if this
case demanded more of His assistance somehow. "I
don't know how the lady will react to this."

She was entering her living room, cup of tea in hand,
with a bewildered look, obviously surprised to see me
back.

"Are you a Christian?" I asked.

"I'm Catholic."

"Then you believe in Jesus Christ and His healing
power," I continued.

A look of skepticism stole across her face as she stood there, still holding her cup of tea. I supposed she was wondering who this strange man could be. I assured her I'd pray for her healing, whatever her need, then be on my way. She lowered her cup and saucer to a stand and I took her frail, shaking hands. My prayer was simple, but a warmth enveloped us. I watched a peace soften the lines in her face.

Then, in her distinct Hungarian accent, she rapidly began telling me of her earlier life as a motorcycle racer in Hungary. "Come, see my trophies," she commanded, and pulled out pictures to verify the gold statues in front of me. I then shared that my two sons and I had been into motocross at one time, and I'd even owned a track. So her excitement heightened when I shared my interest with her.

"Come with me," she again instructed, grabbing a key. I followed her out the door to the first motel room. The knotty pine paneling gave the room a coziness I liked.

"Is this all right?" she questioned.

"What do you mean, 'Is this all right?' "

"Would this room satisfy you?"

"It's beautiful," I assured her.

"It's yours," she said, handing me the key, though mentioning nothing of the rate. I imagined the price to be much beyond the twenty dollars we could spend.

Perhaps twenty minutes had passed while the car still ran with its door open. June's puzzled look demanded an explanation when I told her we'd be spending the night there. I shared everything that had happened.

Next we wondered where we could get a good meal. I'd savored the thought of tasting juicy, tender pork chops for dinner. My new Hungarian friend named a nearby Friendly restaurant which she said specialized in delicious family meals. I rather doubted her word again, but June and I set off to find the place she'd recommended.

It was just as she'd said, family-style, attractive, with a full menu. One look at the choices and I smiled with the knowledge that God was directing us, even to the right restaurant. The specialty of the evening was pork chops, and for only a bit over three dollars.

As soon as we arrived back at our room, there was our "friend" again, asking if we'd liked our dinners. It was then I saw that one of her legs was decidedly shorter than the other. I mentioned my observation and spoke of how we'd seen God "grow out" people's legs. I told her He'd performed this miracle for me. She agreeably seated herself in the room's rocking chair. As June and I prayed, immediately the shorter leg was lengthened. The woman, excited at what God had done, jumped from her chair, shot out the door, and began running up and down the cement porch in front of the motel.

But lingering in my mind was the question of how much we'd have to pay for this lovely room. I decided before we spent the night I'd better get my question answered.

"There's no charge," was her reply. "What you've done for me I could never repay."

Our further conversation the next morning revealed a most fascinating eighty-one-year-old woman. An ardent bird-lover, she'd given each bird a name. When she called them one by one, in they flew to eat the seed she offered in her hand.

June and I were filled with gratitude for God's unusual blessing. But now it was time to drive on to Binghamton, New York where I was scheduled to speak.

After checking in at the fine motel where a room had been reserved for us, June and I found a small restaurant on the upper level. When paying, I conversed for a few moments with the ambitious young girl who managed the place, then left.

"Go back and ask that girl if she knows Me," the voice of the Lord commanded as June and I headed for our room. Obediently I turned and went back. It was thrilling when, even with other people nearby, the girl prayed to receive Jesus by the front counter.

Our prayers for a good meeting were answered the next morning. God moved beautifully in many people's lives, saving, healing and delivering. Then we started for home.

"Go to Waverly, New York," God directed a while later as I drove. "But I don't know where it is," I countered. Just then a sign for Waverly greeted me. I shared with June, and she concurred with the direction I'd received.

As we drove through the town, June asked me what I was supposed to do there. I had to admit I had no idea. I drove slowly, looking from left to right for a clue as to what God had in mind.

"God, You got me here. Now show me what I'm to do," I prayed. As we began to leave town, on the other end of the main street I noted a theater-turned-church, next to it a Bible bookstore, and across from these, an antique and junk shop. At that moment, I knew I was to visit both stores. I imagined God had a special item in the antique shop which the church could use. But within five minutes of entering the little shop, I was involved in deep conversation with the owner, a Catholic man. He told me of his son who had just become a charismatic. The man was concerned. Hurrying back to the car, I grabbed my Bible. Then, for nearly half an hour, I explained Scriptures about the born-again experience and the work of the Holy Spirit to this man so he'd know what had happened to his son.

Although he made no personal commitment at that time, I knew he'd been stirred as well as comforted, knowing his son had had an authentic experience in the Lord. Later I learned that many townspeople had this man on their prayer lists.

Next I crossed the street to visit the bookstore, again not knowing the purpose of my mission. I began a conversation with the woman behind the counter.

"I don't know what I'm doing here today," she suddenly blurted out. "I'm not supposed to be here. Besides that, I'm sick."

"I think I know why we're both here," I said, smiling. "God's going to heal you right now."

As I prayed, her sickness left. Just as we finished, the shop door opened and a lady and child entered. Within moments I was praying for the child, who had been ill.

"This is just wonderful!" the first woman exclaimed, bubbling over with joy.

A display of large-print Bibles stood nearby.

"We have these Bibles on special sale," she said, showing me one.

"Yes, they're nice Bibles, but I'm not able to buy one today," I told her, not adding that I'd wanted this type for some time.

"Oh, I don't want to sell you one. I'm giving it to you."

I value the inscription she added to the front, "Pastor, you are truly a man sent from God."

The story wasn't quite finished then, however.

After returning home from our vacation, I lost my glasses. Even though I asked God to help me find them, I couldn't locate them anywhere. The large-print Bible was the only one I could read well, so I was especially grateful for this gift.

Over two months later, not yet finding the glasses, I gave up my search.

As I sat in my study one day, I tried to read the small print in my Strong's Concordance. Finally, exasperated, I closed the book.

"Lord, I'm asking you to do one of two things," I

prayed. "Either heal my eyes so I can see up close with 20/20 vision, or help me find my glasses."

Suddenly, I was motivated to step outside and walk along the edge of the church parking lot. I walked directly to a particular clump of grass, reached under it, and there were my glasses, still in the case. Although dirty, they were intact, even though cars had parked in that area for two months.

We thanked the Lord for the results of that trip: five nights of free lodging, miracles of salvation and healing, and I had a beautiful new Bible, too.

**\* \* \* \* \* \* \***

It was a miserable, rainy night, and I was scheduled to speak at a Full Gospel Businessmen's dinner. My feelings matched the weather. I was down, feeling empty. Still, I spoke the same message as usual, recounting the amazing things God is doing today.

"We will see them," I assured the listeners. "Many will say, 'I don't believe,' but really mean, 'I believe.'"

At the close, a long line of people waited for prayer. Two of the chapter's officers asked me, however, if I'd pray first for a woman in the back of the room. She'd been in two auto accidents and was horribly bent over, her whole body crooked from the injuries she'd suffered.

"In two minutes you won't feel any pain," were the words which burst unchecked from my lips.

I next took her hands and carefully lifted her twisted body. As I began to pray, she went over in the Spirit. I followed her, keeping one hand on her forehead. Suddenly, all of us who had gathered around her heard a tremendous cracking and watched as her body righted itself, bones jerking into correct position. For several moments the motion continued. When the evidence of healing was complete, this restored woman began singing and dancing around the room.

It was, indeed, the most dramatic healing I'd ever seen.

A woman stood nearby, her head bent to the left, locked by arthritis in her neck.

"Be healed in Jesus' Name," I commanded, touching her head. Immediately it shot upright into normal position.

"I don't believe..." she began, as everyone laughed, and she jumped in elation.

At another FGBMFI meeting, I'd already prayed for many people when an elderly woman approached me, desiring prayer. Her problem: crippling arthritis.

As I laid one hand on her, the Lord gave me a Word of knowledge.

"Do you have unforgiveness in your heart?" I asked.

"Yes, I do," she quickly answered.

"You know you've got to forgive them."

"I never will," she brusquely replied.

I shared how Jesus forgave, painting a word picture of Him standing before the soldiers. I graphically told how they'd mocked, spit on Him, jammed thorns on His head; yet He never uttered a word. After several moments of sharing, I waited for her positive reply, a readiness to forgive.

Instead she said, "What they've done to me I can never forgive."

"Then ma'am, you're going straight to hell!" I shouted, pointing a finger at her startled face. I, too, was amazed at my strong words. I knew the Holy Spirit had spoken.

Suddenly, fear-filled eyes stared back into mine.

"Then I'll ask forgiveness," she hastily answered.

When I prayed, she was freed, not only from unforgiveness, but arthritis as well.

# Chapter Twenty-six

# Called to the World

*"Declare his glory among the heathen; his marvellous works among all nations. For great is the Lord, and greatly to be praised: he also is to be feared above all gods"* (I Chron. 16:24, 25).

I was seated in a large banqueting hall at Earlham College with nearly six hundred others, attending a National Yokefellow Conference. The year was 1963.

As I lounged and conversed with others at one table, a two-year-old boy approached me. I noted his neat little dark suit and tie as he politely greeted me and extended a hand to shake mine.

Later that evening, over twenty conferees gathered in a campus home to share what Jesus Christ was doing in their lives. Among them were the boy's parents, Jean and Neil Biteler, and with them was Mark, the son I'd already met.

Before the evening's end, Mark had blessed us with a lusty rendition of "Jesus Loves Me." An eighty-two-year-old gentleman joined him on the second verse. Through spiritual eyes God let me see two children raising their voices together in praise. I felt privileged to be part of such a holy, inspiring moment.

That began my friendship with the Bitelers.

Sixteen years later I received a phone call from Jean. Would I call Mark, she asked, now a student at the University of Illinois, and encourage him? He seemed overwhelmed with struggles with both his studies and his faith.

I was happy to call, and after a good conversation, Mark and I prayed together. Then, with Christmas near, he asked if he could come spend the holiday with our family. He wanted to talk further and have us pray for him. Mark arrived, and a day or two later a few of us joined for prayer in the living room.

Jesus' Presence filled the room, baptizing Mark in His Spirit. As he lay sprawled on the floor under the Spirit's anointing, he began praying in a heavenly language. For some time he continued, enjoying this beautiful experience.

Suddenly he rose from the floor and, placing his hands on various ones in the gathering, spoke words of prophecy. Not knowing the persons, Mark also couldn't know the veracity of his words. But I did, and with me it established the credibility of what was happening. It was adequate preparation for what God did next.

"My son, my son," He spoke through Mark, as the young man laid his hands on me. "You will be going into the whole world for Me. You will be ministering My Word in many new places."

Abraham's Sarah popped to mind as the import of the words settled over me. I thought of how she'd laughed when told she'd have a baby at ninety years of age, and I began laughing at the preposterous words Mark had just spoken.

"WHY DO YOU QUESTION ME?" came the sharp rebuke from my own lips. Fear quickly replaced laughter. I didn't doubt God's ability, only His choice of vessel. My ministry and I seemed greatly insignificant for such a large task.

In Joel 2:28 we read, "And it shall come to pass

afterward, that I will pour out my spirit upon all flesh; and your sons and your daughters shall prophesy, your old men shall dream dreams, your young men shall see visions." This was happening.

Nearly a year later I got a call from Carlton Spencer, President of Elim Fellowship, asking if I wanted a man from India to speak at our Sunday evening service. I did, welcoming any opportunity to hear what God was doing in another part of the world.

Pastor P. Philip of Madras, South India had a powerful testimony to share of how his wife, a Christian, had committed herself to fasting and prayer for him while he sat in a hotel room, fatally ill and planning suicide. But Jesus appeared to Philip, healed him and forgave his sins. He headed home, a changed man. It was a thrilling recounting and filled with God's power.

At the close, several of us gathered in front of the chapel's fireplace for quiet prayer. Both Brother Philip and I began to pray in the Spirit. Suddenly we realized we were speaking the same language, word for word, a different language than either of us had heard before. We gazed at each other, certain that God had something special planned. He brought a beautiful oneness of His Spirit between us.

"Someday you'll be in India," Brother Philip spoke with finality before leaving. His words penetrated my heart as I remembered how, years before, I'd told God that if He ever sent me anywhere in the world, it wouldn't be India. I'd read of the heat, contaminated food and water, the poverty, the cobras, and figured there were other places He could ask me to go. But I also thought of Mark's prophecy and knew Brother Philip's words held truth.

He returned to India. I continued ministering in Canandaigua, the words tucked away in a recess of my mind.

Nearly a year passed when one day I unearthed a

lovely card Philip had sent after his visit. To frame a reply, I lay the card on my desk.

When Brother Philip called a few days later, I wasn't surprised. Excitement filled my voice on learning he was just a few miles away, near Rochester. He said he'd been led by God to come.

Philip accepted my immediate invitation and the next day I brought him to our home. For over six weeks we fellowshipped.

The first night, as our son Jim, Philip and I met at our kitchen table for prayer, we joined hands. Soon God gave me a vision. I saw the world surrounded with blackness. But as I viewed this dark globe there appeared a brilliant light shining in America, then in India. Soon I saw brilliant lights shining from spots all over the world. Next the lights moved, joining together in a ribbon of light encircling the globe. The lights wove around each other until a web of light surrounded the earth.

The Lord spoke then and gave me an understanding of the vision.

"The lights shining from different parts of the world are those people who have taken the light of Jesus Christ," He informed me. "And His light is shining through them. They are now being joined around the world."

Next He said Satan would try to cut these cords of light, but that he wouldn't be able to separate or break them. Quickly the Scripture from Romans eight came to mind — that nothing shall separate us from the love of God.

As I studied the light, I heard God's voice speak again. "I am putting My people together, My Church, to come and bring them unto Myself." With that, our prayer time ended.

In travels since, I've met those all over the world with Christ's light burning in them. I've sensed God welding us to shine as one, linked in a bond the world can't break.

Two years later, when Philip visited us again, he and I attended a regional FGBMFI convention in Portland, Maine. A lady approached us after one of the meetings.

"God has put you together," she said. "You will minister, sometimes in great danger." She saw protecting angels on our right and left.

Philip confirmed her words. During a prayer time in India, he and others had asked God who their speaker should be at special services they'd planned. God gave them the name "Jack Moore," he said. No fleece was necessary this time. God had spoken and confirmed his words.

So Philip began to plan an itinerary for my first visit to India in 1981. I marvelled, but no more did I question. I knew if God calls, He also equips. He can do all things through us if we place ourselves at His disposal. Still, I wanted to ask God about our plans.

"Do you mind," I asked Philip, "If I go to the woods to pray and hear what the Lord says?" He didn't mind, of course.

As I began praying, I asked God for a Word. Through my own mouth He spoke.

"My son, my Son. You can know it is I who am sending you into the world, for hasn't this been prophesied?" He asked. "When prophecies are fulfilled, aren't they of Me?" He continued to speak words of encouragement.

As usual, I wanted scriptural confirmation, so I opened the Bible I'd carried. I read First Chronicles 16:24: "Declare his glory among the heathen; his marvellous works among all nations." Then I read verse twenty-five: "...[God] also is to be feared above all gods."

I pictured cobras and fear gripped me. I knew snakes are worshiped in India.

Looking up, I had a vision of God. Next to Him was an ugly, hooded king cobra, ready to strike me.

"Whom do you fear?"

"Why You, Lord, of course," I replied, as fear drained from me.

"You'll be all right; you'll be all right," He reassured me.

I wasn't tormented again by any fear of outside forces, especially snakes. And now I was certain He was sending me to other parts of the world to serve Him and declare His glory.

A few days later, as Mark Biteler, June and I joined in prayer, we fell to our knees under God's power. Tongues and interpretation came to me.

"I'm not sending you to India to leave or forsake you," God assured me. "I'll never leave you. You'll have a difficult time. Your faith will be tested. But I'm not sending you to India to leave you there. You'll come home to your family."

His words helped sustain me during those difficult testings in India the following year, February of 1981.

# Chapter Twenty-seven

# Pastor Philip

*"For whosoever will save his life shall lose it; but whosoever shall lose his life for my sake and the gospel's, the same shall save it"* (Mark 8:35).

Philip was born into an idol-worshiping family in the village of Gopinenipalem and was dedicated to the cobra god. A cobra tattooed on his forehead was a reminder of this.

His three older sisters had died of a disease. Suddenly Philip, at three months of age, was dying of the same dreaded disease.

One day, many boys from a town several miles away were playing in the hills when one fell, breaking a leg. A Christian man, exiled by angry villagers for preaching Jesus, heard the boys crying. Coming from the woods, he prayed for the boy and he was healed.

Now the village people sought out the man they'd stoned. He prayed for them and their children. Because of the many miracles they saw, multitudes received Jesus.

When Philip's parents heard of this Christian, they wanted him to pray for Philip.

The worried mother and father carried Philip to the

"saint," as he was called now. "If you will dedicate this boy to Jesus Christ and the Lord's ministry," he instructed, holding Philip in his arms, "he'll be healed." Although they didn't understand the conditions he'd set, in desperation they obeyed and Philip was healed. The Christian then changed the baby's name from Pullayya, "dedicated to the cobra god," to Philip.

For a time his parents walked forty-four miles to see the "saint." They also ridded their home of idols. But, having no Bible, they couldn't learn about this God who had saved their son.

"If you ever get into trouble," Philip's mother had told him, "Call on the Name of Jesus."

When he was fourteen, his mother died. His father then married a heathen woman who brought twenty-some idols back into the house.

A hatred developed between Philip and his step-mother. One morning, when he was sixteen, he sat to eat his ration of rice. When some of the household's cats clamored for food, he stuck some into the mouth of one cat. In moments it was dead.

Philip tore from the house. "My stepmother's trying to kill me," he yelled.

When his father returned home, he didn't believe Philip's recounting. Instead, he listened to his wife who said that because the boy hated her, he poisoned his own food, then blamed her.

"She's not trying to poison you. You're just a crazy kid wanting to shame our family," his father declared. "Get out of my house. I don't ever want to see you again!"

Philip, crying, ran to his mother's grave. There he dropped in grief and for many hours he begged, "Mother, come and help me or send Jesus Christ." But no one appeared. Then he called on all the Hindu gods. Still there was no answer or help. Now Philip declared himself an atheist.

He began walking the forty-four miles to Vijaya-
wada and entered a boys' military training group.
Later he was promoted into the regular army.

During his military career, the India-China War
broke out. He left to fight. During an attack, every man
but Philip was killed. Everywhere he looked he saw
dead bodies. He lay still, afraid the least movement
would alert the enemy plane overhead. After dark,
Philip crawled up into a tree, certain the enemy would
return.

He perched quietly, high in the branches, for two or
three days while enemy forces returned, checking the
dead. Finally, when the area was still again, Philip
carefully lowered himself to the ground and turned
toward home.

Now he desired marriage. However, with his parents
dead, Philip had no one to arrange a marriage for him
according to Indian custom. When a family offered him
their daughter, he accepted.

"She's too black," was his thought when he saw her
for the first time at their ceremony. "What will I do?
There's no escape."

The marriage took place as planned, however, and
on the third day afterward Lilly was brought to Philip,
according to another Indian custom. Immediately
Philip saw the Bible she carried, a symbol of her belief
in God. Lilly's father, Philip learned, was a Lutheran
pastor. "Lady, I don't like you and I don't like your
Bible," Philip roughly declared as she stood before
him. He grabbed the book and tore it up to emphasize
his own disbelief.

When a daughter was born to them, Philip liked his
wife a bit better because the baby resembled his
mother. Then a son was born with some of his father's
features, so he liked Lilly even better. In all, ten
children would grace their home.

By this time Philip had entered police work, and for
the next thirteen years was a police inspector. His
successful pursuit of criminals earned him the respect

of police officials. He was cited for his undercover work in solving many difficult cases in his part of India.[1]

Meanwhile, Lilly began to teach in a Pentecostal school and was filled with the Holy Spirit. The first time Philip heard his wife praying in tongues, he slapped her across the mouth. "Stop that foolishness," he shouted.

Philip gambled much of their money. Then a hard life of drinking (he'd become an alcoholic) and smoking took its toll. Philip began bleeding in his lungs and his heart was severely enlarged. With only three or four months to live, according to the doctors, Philip decided to take his life.

He demanded all the money his wife had saved from her teaching and left for Madras City. "There's hope in Jesus," Lilly had said, but he couldn't believe her.

After buying eighteen bottles of brandy, several tins of cigarettes and a bottle of potent poison, he rented a hotel room. Several days later, the brandy and cigarettes gone, Philip reached for the poison. But something physically stopped him.

When her husband had left, Lilly said in prayer, "You are the living God. You're able to bring back my husband alive, so I'm not going to eat or drink until You bring him home."

Five others joined her in prayer for five days, then gave up. They advised her to stop, too. "He's probably already dead and the government's buried him," they said.

"I don't care. I've believed in the Jesus that raised Lazarus from the dead. So if Philip's already dead, I expect Jesus to raise him and bring him back to me," Lilly replied resolutely.

1. During one of my trips to India, I was happy to see a police journal in which Philip was lauded for his excellent police work. The Hindu police force now delcared him to be "one of the most authentic Christians we know."

Meanwhile, when his hand couldn't reach the poison, Philip knew a Power filled the room. He cried out for help. Suddenly, a fiery light appeared in the room, and its power knocked him to the floor.

"Is there any God? Come and help me," he cried out. Looking up, he saw Jesus, arms outstretched toward him, and heard a voice.

"My son, My son, I have chosen you for My ministry," were the words Philip heard.

"Lord, I'm a sinner. I'm unholy; I'm sick," Philip cried. "When my wife told me about You, I didn't believe."

"But I've forgiven you," Jesus lovingly said.

Although light covered Jesus' face, Philip could see His bleeding body. Suddenly he felt a drop of blood touch his chest. Instantly he was healed and filled with the Holy Spirit. The tongues he'd been so opposed to now flowed automatically from his mouth. He headed for home at once.

Approaching the house, he could hear Lilly still praying, so he quietly knocked. So shining and filled with God's glory was her face because of the days of prayer and fasting that he thought an angel greeted him.

"Angel, I won't let go till you bless me," Philip begged, dropping to his knees and wrapping his arms around her legs.

"Oh, thank you, God," Lilly prayed. "You've brought my husband home."

Now he knew the shining being was his wife.

Through the night they knelt together in prayer, thanking and seeking God. About five a.m., the same light Philip saw in his hotel room appeared in their home. It rested on their sleeping seven-year-old daughter. She immediately awakened and began speaking in tongues.

"My son, My son," God spoke through the young girl, "You will be going into the world to serve Me."

Since that time Philip has visited over thirty countries, testifying to Jesus' saving power.

And the cobra tatoo remains on his forehead as further testimony that God brought him from death to new life.

*******

Philip's portico, with the moon still visible in the early morning, proved to be a perfect place for prayer, I found during my first trip to India. The noise at other times made thoughtful prayer an impossibility.

One morning as I prayed and walked on the portico, I was suddenly conscious of a person walking with me. I quickly noted the sackcloth, a burlap-type material, of the seamless robe He wore.

"I am raising Philip up for a mighty work," He said with great authority. "Tell him to remain humble."

With the warmth that flowed through me came the knowledge that this was Christ speaking. I turned, but He was gone.

When I passed the Word on to Philip we wept together, knowing God would mightily use him if he kept his integrity and humility.

"Why were You wearing sackcloth?" I asked the Lord later as I reflected on His appearance.

"Because I'm so grieved for the lost, and the time is so short," I heard in my spirit.

It increased my desire to bring them to Jesus.

# Chapter Twenty-eight

# A Lesson in Patience

*"And beside this, giving all diligence, add to your ... knowledge temperance; and to temperance patience ..."* (II Pet. 1:5-6).

As I waited in New York to fly to India, I asked God for a Word. "In your patience possess ye your soul," I heard (Luke 21:19). Those words would often ring in my mind in the next hours. "Oh, God, this promises to be a test of my patience," I complained, already impatient with a delay.

I reached Germany for an hour and a half stopover, and a pastor friend, Herrmann Dallmann, asked me to take an accordion to India. A member of his congregation had given it to missions. I already had two wooden lockers filled with clothes to give away, plus all my own luggage. I thought of the help I'd have, however, when I reached India. Philip was sending a friend to help me through customs in Bombay and also to help me catch my flight for Madras City. But sickness, I later learned, kept him from coming.

The hot air was foul-smelling as I deplaned in Bombay. I felt a thick oppression blanketing the area like black storm clouds. Much rain before my arrival now added to the sticky humidity and mosquitoes were everywhere.

Thousands of brown bodies filled the terminal, an oversized gymnasium-type building. I pulled and hauled the heavy pieces of luggage while searching the sea of faces for someone who would recognize me as the tall white missionary from the United States. But no one claimed me or my burdens.

I chose one line of the many people waiting to go through customs after being checked through immigration. Red and green lights on the wall ahead meant nothing to me. For half an hour I pushed the two lockers and accordion and carried two large suitcases and a shoulder bag while inching toward the customs official.

"Sir, you can go to the green line," an English-speaking Indian instructed, pointing to another line. So again I pushed the lockers with my feet and hefted the other heavy cases. Finally, in another half hour I reached the customs officer. His check was routine until he came to the accordion.

"What is this?" he asked with a curious look.

"An accordion," I replied.

"You will have to pay customs tax on this," he stated. Getting out his thick book of information, he checked and conferred with other officials, while I stood for another half hour.

"Is this a new or used accordion?" he queried.

I didn't know.

"That will be five hundred rupees," (about fifty dollars), he said simply.

I gulped, knowing I had no extra funds for such an expense, while he checked all my other items. By the time he'd finished his inspection, somehow he and I had both forgotten about the accordion, and I was pushed on.

By now I was exhausted, having left home Thursday afternoon. It was Saturday, 2:30 a.m. The travel, the bewilderment and the excitement had left me drained. How I hoped someone would rescue me, but still there was no one. I'd have to get myself to the domestic airport five miles away to catch my flight for Madras City.

As I dragged myself into the crowds outside, barefoot children rushed to grab my bags, anxious to earn a few rupees. Two were successful.

I needed a bus, only to find there were none. A taxi was available, and after loading all my baggage into the little car, the driver, his helper and I wove our way through the streets for the twenty-minute ride to the next airport. I whispered a prayer for God's help as we twisted and turned onto one street, then another. I was apprehensive, my mind creating horrid pictures of being robbed. But finally we ended up at the second airport.

Before embarking, I'd agreed on the price of ten rupees, or one dollar, for the taxi ride. However, upon our arrival, the driver and his friend, stretching hands in front of me, demanded ten dollars. I stated the original price while they angrily yelled theirs. Too tired to argue further, I handed them the money. In subsequent trips to India, I never again gave in. I learned to say no.

I'd arrived in India at one-thirty a.m. It was now about three. Sleep was my first thought. My flight wouldn't leave until seven, so I had time to rest, I figured. I sank down, all my belongings around me, and leaned my head back, grateful I'd gotten this far in my journey.

"I advise you, sir, not to go to sleep, or all your bags will be stolen." A man's voice spoke with a clear accent.

I opened my eyes to find an Australian standing before me. "There's a hotel about a half mile away," he added, and suggested I get a room until my flight time.

I thanked him for his help, and after checking some of my baggage, found a young man to help carry the rest for the short walk to the hotel. Upon arriving, the boy asked for two hundred rupees. I reminded him we'd settled on fifty and handed him that amount. I was getting smarter.

As I made out the necessary passport form to register, I anxiously asked, "How much is a room?"

"Five hundred rupees," the manager answered.

"Sir, I'm a man of God. He provides my money and He wouldn't want me spending fifty dollars for three hours."

"There is our lobby," he said, pointing. "It has dividers and there are guards. Go over and go to sleep. It'll be all right."

Toting my belongings to the lobby, I plunked down on a couch. "God, what's going on?" I asked. "I'm exhausted; I'm in a strange land; the man who was supposed to meet me wasn't here; I was cheated and lied to; I feel the oppression, and I have no bed."

Just then I heard keys rattling and opened my eyes. There stood the manager before me.

"Sir, somebody just checked out of a room which has two beds and two sets of towels," he informed me. "There will be a clean bed and one clean set of towels for you. Our man will help you up to the room with your luggage. You can take a bath and sleep until your flight. We won't charge you."

I thanked him and the Lord for the accommodations, the nicest I ever found during my trips to India.

After a refreshing shower, I plopped onto the bed, exhausted, yet afraid to sleep because of my flight schedule. So I kept waking to check the time. At six-thirty a.m. I was up, ready to catch India Air.

I arrived back at the airport, only to find the flight delayed. Later in the morning an announcer invited all waiting passengers to a free lunch in the airport's restaurant, serving, I thought, both American and Indian foods. There I saw, though, an extensive buffet of Indian cuisine. Having been warned of the hot

Indian curries, I found an English-speaking businessman nearby who agreed to guide me in my selections. He would tell me whether the dishes were hot or not. With my first forkful of rice with curry, I felt as if a match had been lighted in my mouth. He'd called this mild! I couldn't wait to fill my mouth with the grainy "ice cream" served for dessert. My "guide" graciously gave me his, too.

Finally, after waiting all afternoon as well, my plane left at six p.m., arriving in Madras about eight. By now my eyes fought to stay open. Thankfully, Philip met me.

Every American or European I knew visiting India that year became sick, and many were hospitalized. Several Baptist evangelists I met had all been in the hospital. One sick woman was sent home and later died. When I contracted fever, upset stomach and diarrhea, Philip had his doctor visit me four times.

"I already have a Doctor," I told the kind physician and Philip. "He told me He'd bring me back home safely. If you can just show me some way to keep this food down, I'll be okay." I refused the prescriptions, sensing that I was to use my faith instead. But weakness made getting off my cot a terrible chore. Several times I heard Philip's wife, Lilly, slip quietly into my room to kneel and pray. They thought I was going to die, but I was clinging to God's promise to me.

Once I managed to kneel by my cot. As I prayed I heard God's voice speak: "Go home and tell My people there will be suffering, and they will be tested as you're being tested now, before the end comes. Tell them to remain strong."

One day I told Philip, "I can't preach tonight. I'm too sick." But in a few minutes I changed my words. "I'll be there if you have to carry me," I spoke with new resolve. "Satan isn't getting the victory."

In the following days I ministered the Word and prayed for people, but weakness enveloped me afterward. Once, when I'd preached for an hour, I wanted Philip to take over.

"You must go on," he said. "I'm sick, too."

I prayed for nearly two hundred people. Many received healings while I felt increasingly sick. Excusing myself, I ran out into the field, a dangerous thing to do at night because of the cobras. But my upset stomach overcame my fear. I returned and ministered until all who desired it received prayer.

At the next meeting place I was sick again. "Philip, this will kill me," I said weakly, from a bed in the hotel room we'd just rented. There were no air-conditioned rooms available and the temperature hovered between 110 and 120 degrees. He left immediately and found a second-class hotel room on the beach by the Indian Ocean. It had a half-working air-conditioner. The half, however, provided some relief from the oppressive heat and humidity.

Later in the afternoon as I sat in the hotel's dining room to have a "lemca" (an Indian lemon-lime drink), I glanced up to see a huge rat headed toward me. But it ran by my feet and scurried away. (Since they're considered sacred, rats flourish there.)

As Philip and I returned to Madras he made a welcome suggestion. "I'll take you to Spencer's" (a large store featuring American and European goods) "and buy you some American food."

I was delighted with his idea. But Philip never had a chance to go. The grocery department burned to the ground that night. To us, it underscored the spiritual battle we were waging.

My visa was for one month, but because Philip knew all the officials, he could easily obtain an extension for me. One day he set out to do that. While he was gone, I went to my knees.

"God, You either heal me or send me home," I prayed. "I can't go any further." Two weeks of meetings were left, but I wondered how I'd ever make it, minus a miracle, if I stayed.

Soon the phone rang. It was Philip. "I can't get your visa renewed," he said, puzzled at the difficulty. "In two days you have to be at the Bombay airport." I arrived at the airport in the early morning hours, the midday heat making take-offs impossible.

"I've been in India for a month," I informed the steward upon boarding, "and I need a ginger ale or 7-Up. Could I please have one?"

Although it wasn't their policy to serve drinks before take-off, he understood my need and accommodated me. As I stood sipping an ice-cold ginger ale, tears streamed down my face. Never had the bubbly drink tasted so good.

I'd lost thirty pounds in thirty-one days, and was thankful to be alive. Thankful, too, to be heading home.

*******

In 1982 June and one of the church elders accompanied me to India. Philip had set up a week of meetings at Madras City in the orphanage compound. Seven to eight hundred people attended each night. Chairs had been rented for these high-caste people from the city. In fact, it was the only time we ever had chairs for our services.

Our next meetings were scheduled for Nellore, hometown of a communist who had been converted and had begun a church.

The day before leaving I started running a fever and had "motions," an Indian idiom for a quivery stomach. June and I prayed and I was fine on the train trip.

However, when we arrived at our hotel late at night, the fever and stomach problem started again. At one a.m. June agreed with me in prayer as I paced the room, praying for God to heal me and give direction. I was puzzled, since some of the Christians here had had a word that I wouldn't be sick in India again. I was contrasting the word with my feelings.

Suddenly, as I neared one corner of the room, the Lord spoke to me from Deuteronomy 8:3: "I have caused you to be hungry so you'd know that man shall not live by bread alone, but by every word that proceedeth from the mouth of God. I now want you to eat only when and what I tell you."

I understood Him to mean that I was to fast until He indicated otherwise. "Lord, I'll do it," I responded, and immediately the fever and all signs of sickness left. I was healed. I realized if I was faithful to this Word, I'd not be sick in India again.

Even after fasting for three days, I felt wonderful. Then I was on a partial fast, with God instructing me to eat no meat, chicken or fish. I could eat rice, vegetables, a few fruits, and could drink some milk or tea, all as He directed me. I called it a Daniel fast, remembering God's instructions to him in Scripture.

I learned to drink the Indian coffee, made with half buffalo milk and loaded with coarse sugar. I found that a hot beverage, even in the torrid climate, protected my throat when speaking. In fact, I became accustomed to drinking all my beverages hot, including milk, the way the Indians do.

I appreciated the practicality of God's instructions. Never again was I sick during any of my travels in India.

# Chapter Twenty-nine

# Ministry in India

*"He shall cover thee with his feathers, and under his wings shalt thou trust: his truth shall be thy shield and buckler"* (Ps. 91:4).

During my first missionary trip God manifested His power in mighty ways, with hundreds coming to Jesus and many baptized in the Holy Ghost. God also manifested His power through healings and deliverances wherever we went.

The Indian people who accept Jesus call themselves "believers," not "Christians." They associate the word "Christian" with those who attend church on Sunday, but fail during the week to live out their commitment to Jesus Christ. Many of them smoke, drink and gamble. I learned also that they often cheat and lie in their business dealings.

However, "believers," according to the Indian people, are those who have accepted Jesus Christ, believe in the fulness of His power, and live by His example.

I was reminded of Mark's Gospel, the sixteenth chapter, where Jesus speaks of believers. Those who believe, He said, would be saved. Then signs would follow as earmarks of their belief in Him.

The third meeting of our missionary tour was held in the small village of Pithapuram. With no place to stay, we trusted the Lord to take care of us. A Christian nurse, learning of our situation, gave us her home on the hospital grounds and moved her family onto the front porch.

Next we took a room in Kakinada, nearly twenty-five kilometers (ten to fifteen miles) from the following meeting place. It was a new hotel, still under construction, with no hot water or kitchen facilities yet. We found this to be usual in India.

The first two nights we traveled by taxi. However, besides being expensive, it was harrowing, with drivers tearing crazily down the roads, dodging animals and people.

The buses were slightly better, only because they were cheaper. Designed to hold about forty-five people, they'd be jammed with one hundred or more. Several chickens were often added.

On the outside of the bus would hang several young men, clinging to the windows and door frames to hitch rides.

Sticky dark brown bodies clutched large bags in which belongings and food were wrapped. A few children cried from the heat, illness, or maybe hunger. Elbows and feet were everywhere. Nauseating body, food and animal odors all mixed and assaulted my nostrils in the one hundred plus temperatures, making these rides barely tolerable.

We bounced along, springs broken, through deep potholes, around ox carts, pigs, goats and sacred cows. The wandering animals quickly snatched up the garbage tossed out the bus windows.

Often blocking the way were pedestrians, bicyclists, or various hand-drawn vehicles. Sometimes it was other buses, trucks or automobiles that stood in our path.

"Brother, watch your pocket," Philip warned me as

we rode, knowing I was an easy target for thieves in such a crowd. But I had no fear.

"Philip, we can't take the bus back tonight," I announced on the last night of meetings in Pithapuram. Philip looked puzzled.

"We must not take the bus tonight," I repeated, more emphatically. I knew I'd had a leading from the Lord.

"We have to take the bus," Philip insisted. But I held firmly to the instinct I was sure God had given me.

"How are we to travel back?" he queried, still bewildered.

"We must get a car."

"But there won't be any cars there," he answered. "It's a small village and there won't be any automobiles for hire."

I was certain that under no condition could we ride the return bus.

When we arrived at the meeting site, Philip and a co-worker walked to a nearby gas station where they found a brand new light green car parked.

"Do you need an automobile?" the car's driver asked. He had to return to Kakinada, but had no gasoline. Philip immediately hired him at a very reasonable price, supplying him with money for the needed gas, and then brought him along to the meeting ground, parking the car nearby.

The headlines in the morning paper quickly informed us why God had changed our normal plans. "Bus Hits Guardrail, Tips Over, Goes Into Water," the headlines read. Sixty-seven bodies had been pulled from the water so far. We felt great sorrow for those who had died, but gratitude for God's protection.

Wherever we went, many spiritual attacks accompanied our meetings, attended by fifteen hundred to two thousand. But we were led by the Spirit to always take authority in the Name of Jesus.

In our first meeting at Guntur in south-central India, as I stood to speak the Lord led me strongly to take authority over any evil within the place and to bind the lips of anyone who would come against the meetings.

Later I learned that a communist leader with some of his comrades had come to disrupt the meeting by challenging my authority. Local pastors, recognizing him, watched nervously. When he tried to interfere, he seemed unable to speak. As I preached, the communist's interest grew.

It was our policy at the close of each meeting to lay hands on everyone who wanted prayer. This night was no exception and we began laying hands on all who came forward in the large field where we'd gathered. The communist leader found himself strangely pulled into the prayer line. He'd been suffering from a cancerous gastric ulcer and was unable to eat without severe pain. God led me to lay my hand on his stomach as he walked by and say simply, "In the Name of Jesus."

Intrigued by what he'd heard, he returned the second night, bringing his wife. After five nights of meetings we moved on to another city, but he had attended every service.

The man returned to his village of Nellore and visited his doctor when the meetings were through. After examining him, the doctor said the ulcer was totally gone. The communist found it hard to believe, so he visited seven other doctors who told him the same thing: no ulcer. By then he was convinced that something strange had happened at the first meeting he'd attended. His mind, however, had difficulty believing in the healing power of Jesus Christ and that it was for today.

Curious to learn more, he visited the area pastors, who told him of Jesus. He accepted Him as his Lord and Savior and was baptized in water. It was then his desire to see a church started in his town, so he asked that Brother Philip send a pastor for this purpose.

During our second trip to India in 1982, we found a church of two hundred members in that place. God not only had protected us from interference in that initial service, but in His love had transformed a man and used him as a missionary to his village. In subsequent trips I found this former communist official to be a strong believer and follower of Jesus Christ.

# Chapter Thirty

# More Miracles

*"Heal the sick, cleanse the lepers, raise the dead, cast out devils: freely ye have received, freely give"* (Matt. 10:8).

A large field was leased in Avadi, a suburb of Madras City, for a series of services. Since two languages are spoken there, Tellegu and Tamil, I needed two interpreters every time I spoke.

My visa had run out, so this was the last meeting I could conduct in 1981. God demonstrated His power, just as in the previous meetings, saving and healing many, as well as baptizing them in His Holy Spirit.

A doctor who was a believer had come to the meetings. When he saw the healings, he approached me. Speaking excellent English, he said, "I have brought many of my patients here tonight." Then he proceeded to introduce me to each one in turn, telling me the ailment: stomach problem, asthma, and so on. As each came and the doctor identified the problem, we'd lay hands on him and pray. Several of the doctor's patients were healed that night.

The following year when I returned to conduct meetings at Avadi the doctor was one of the first men to come forward to share with everyone the good news of the many who were healed the year before.

Therefore I was sad to learn during my 1983 trip that because of unrest among the Muslims, Hindus and Christians, many people had been killed, homes burned and vehicles destroyed. We were told if we spoke there we'd be "smashed" (killed). The authorities allowed us only one meeting and provided police protection. God took care of us, as always, allowing us to speak boldly the message of Jesus Christ. Many were saved, healed and baptized in the Holy Ghost.

God proved again that He'll protect and empower us when we're operating under His commission.

In 1982 God took us into the remote village of Sankavarum, where no white preachers had ever been. Because we had to stay so far away (two solid hours of hectic driving), it wasn't possible to conduct teachings in the afternoons. In our absence, a young Indian pastor with good intentions chided the people for their foolishness in following their gods.

The Indian people have intense beliefs. We who ministered together felt responsible to tell them that they didn't have to find God — that He has already found them through Jesus Christ. Neither did we believe it was our place to try to lead them from one religion to another. We taught, and teach, that Jesus never came to establish a religion, but rather a relationship between us and His Father. God has given us the wisdom to share that background doesn't matter; that Jesus Christ is for everyone. Then when people see the signs and wonders they can know that Jesus Christ is Lord.

So, because of the unwise words of the pastor, the villagers were angered. When we arrived that evening, the mayor came with his people to tell us we couldn't conduct any more meetings. The incensed villagers held rocks and sticks while Pastor Philip carefully explained our real purpose. Still they stood, staring at us with weapons in hand while we proceeded with the service.

I'd just begun to preach when out in the road a crowd assembled, again with sticks, stones and rocks. We knew they intended to kill us. But I preached with no fear, and God suddenly manifested His power. One person after another fell down under the Holy Spirit's anointing. Healings began happening all over. The weapons were dropped and many of the dissenters came forward to receive Jesus.

We asked for testimonies from those whose lives God had touched. The first to stand was a young lady about seventeen years old. She had been deaf and dumb since birth, but Jesus had healed her. She could both hear and speak. Philip spoke words to her from a distance and she repeated them clearly.

The scales had fallen from the eyes of an old blind man. First he'd seen men as trees, just as the man had whose story is recorded in Scripture. After we prayed again, however, he could see men as men.

A woman who had been lame ran to the platform; a man whose knees previously wouldn't bend was now kneeling, then standing, kneeling and standing; an asthmatic man who could scarcely breathe before was now jumping and rejoicing in the Lord; a lady who had had twelve years of bleeding was completely healed. On and on the testimonies went.

On the third night June called me over to where she stood with a young woman.

"Do you remember this lady?" June asked me. She then told me how the woman had had leprosy. Her hands had been gnarled and white with the horrible disease. But now, when the woman extended her hands, there was no sign of the leprosy. They were restored to their original color, completely healed.

In Vetlapelam we used an abandoned factory compound for services. It was unusual to have a concrete floor and walls surrounding us; this was the only such place in India where we held services.

We'd mounted a loudspeaker inside and one outside. About fifteen hundred people had come and seated themselves on the floor one night.

A distinct evil presence enveloped us as we began the service. When any of us started to speak, loud voices and murmurings drowned out the sound of our voices. Pastor Philip called me and the other pastors together to join hands and pray. A strong anointing compelled me to take authority over the evil. Philip then prayed with the same anointing, interpreting in Tellegu. Complete, eerie silence reigned as we finished.

The Hindu man operating the sound system had been moving about to cause a distraction; but as we prayed, he jumped up and ran from the building. We never saw him again.

Later we learned that the wall had been surrounded by men, murmuring and intent on creating confusion in the meeting. But God had stilled every voice. There was total silence, and we continued with the service. Many Indians of both high and low caste stood and received Jesus. Demonic spirits and diseases left many. Others were baptized in the Holy Spirit.

As I spoke, a group of men rushed into the building with a man from the fields who had just been bitten by a poisonous snake. Death was certain. (It's estimated that about eight thousand people die each year from cobra bites.) Fear gripped the victim's face as the men interrupted, placing him in front of me on the platform. I prayed for him, then continued with my message. But the Lord spoke to me. "He's still feeling pain." I turned just as one of the interpreters said, "This man is still in pain." The words confirmed that God was in control. As we prayed this time, the pain left. He then received Jesus as Savior.

My thoughts later were of God's divine protection, without which none of us would ever have made it to that place of salvation. Had it not been for God's sovereignty, protection and power, another Indian would have died not knowing Jesus. I rejoiced that this man, instead of being a death statistic, had a life-changing experience with Jesus Christ.

During one of our missionary trips we met a man who attended a night service in the town of Vella. He had had a hip crushed in an accident. The doctors could do nothing for this kind of injury. One leg was nearly five and a half inches shorter than the other. Because of this, he walked with great difficulty.

As we prayed for people that night, the Lord said, "Put this man in a chair on the platform and let these people see My power." So we did, placing him sideways so people could easily view this miracle.

Many times we'd seen short legs grow instantly. But in this case we held his leg for nearly five minutes while praying for God to heal his hip, back and leg. Little by little the leg moved as the people, mouths open, watched God work. Suddenly the miracle was complete. The man jumped to his feet and in his native language of Tellegu told the crowd that Jesus Christ had healed him. He was so excited that the next night he came running to the platform, uninvited, and again told the crowd of the miracle God had performed. How we praised and thanked the Lord for demonstrating His power!

Someone told of seeing fire over our meeting place one afternoon, as if the palm leaves themselves were burning. We knew it was another manifestation of God's power.

God's provision of humor here and there lightened the gravity of our missions in India. We were appreciative.

When June was with me in 1982, for instance, during one evening service she complied with Philip's request to bring initial greetings to the people. As she spoke, suddenly the pendell (a tent-like structure of poles covered with palm leaves) collapsed, spilling palm leaves and branches on the heads of many people. What fun we had teasing her about being a powerful speaker — "bringing down the house."

Then in 1984, Gib Buckbee, a friend from FGBMFI, and I shared an incident which provided laughs for days after.

In one village we stayed in a farmer's house which sported a tiny courtyard — a walled-in area by our cots on the porch. There in the confines of the courtyard we hung our laundry.

One afternoon our attention was drawn to a cavorting monkey on the roof of the house. We remarked about its cuteness as it played with something white.

All at once Gib recognized the cloth. "Those are my shorts!" he shouted, as the monkey pulled and ripped at the undergarment. I laughed heartily while the monkey played.

Seeing our predicament, a native boy grabbed a banana, waved it, then placed the fruit on top of the wall. The monkey scampered for the banana, dropping the torn shorts to the ground. Upon inspection, we found the mischievous animal had left a gaping hole where the seat had been.

While we continued laughing, another monkey scurried to the clothesline and grabbed another piece of clothing — my shorts this time. Fortunately, I retrieved them while they were only soiled. When we arrived back home, on a Sunday morning I made a presentation to Gib — a stuffed monkey. In his grasp I'd placed a white piece of clothing — a pair of ripped shorts.

\* \* \* \* \*

The evangelistic group, including Dick Toulson and me, had checked into the hotel in Adoni, India. Dick had accompanied me on this trip in 1985.

"Jack, this isn't as bad as I'd imagined from all

you've told me," Dick had said earlier. He'd soon learn how distasteful India can be for us soft Americans.

I unpacked my trusty bug spray. Each night on previous visits to India, we'd sprayed around the legs of our beds to avoid painful red ant invasions. Then, so we could use the toilet, we'd sprayed the area first to keep the bugs from attacking our legs. Now I'd do the same.

On my way to the primitive facility (a hole in a raised platform) I noticed a two-inch opening in the concrete under the step out front. Four huge black roaches crawled out. I grimaced and sprayed vigorously. The spray only seemed to serve as an invitation to hundreds of the unwelcome creatures. Soon the whole floor of our room was covered with ugly black bodies.

Dick yelled, dancing furiously, and slapped his leg to rid himself of a roach that had found its way up one pantleg.

With the hotel's more powerful spray, the roaches were killed and the floor swept and washed with a mixture smelling of kerosene and creosote.

Two days later we noticed a growing, horrible odor. Soon it was unbearable. We scoured the room, searching for the source, but found nothing. Then Lilly, Philip's wife, came. She felt directed to look under Dick's bed. There she found the problem — a decomposed bat covered with several roaches. The hotel boy we'd called, picking up the offending animal, tossed it through the screenless window to the pedestrian-filled street below.

Dick shook his head. "Somehow I knew he was going to do that," he commented. He'd quickly learned that, despite the beautiful Indian Christians, ministry in their country could be most difficult.

# Chapter Thirty-one

# Deaf and Dumb Healed

*"When Jesus saw that the people came running together, he rebuked the foul spirit, saying unto him, Thou dumb and deaf spirit, I charge thee, come out of him, and enter no more into him"* (Mark 9:25).

Philip and I jostled along the road to Jaggayyapet in 1983 for the first night of services there, with high expectations of what God would do. We'd fasted and prayed in preparation, knowing the evil spirits we'd encounter.

This would be our third missionary tour together. By now I was well-acquainted with this country filled with strange customs, evil spirits, much disease and death, but filled too with many beautiful, loving people who waited to receive us and the God we'd preach.

We followed a lorry, as these large dump-type trucks are called in India, and approached a sharp curve in the road. Suddenly, another lorry burst into view from the opposite direction, but in our lane. As we watched, we realized neither truck was giving way to the other. Both speeding, they collided head-on. Whole portions of the trucks flew into the air, glass covered the highway, and axles and wheels were ripped off and scattered over the area. The remains of one truck landed off to one side. The other sat in pieces and half-turned in the opposite direction on the highway.

Most frightening, however, was seeing bodies of drivers and riders being thrown in all directions. Because very few people in India own vehicles, people hitch rides on the trucks. I wondered what number lay amongst the wreckage.

We drove through the glass, around the debris and stopped, then ran to see what we could do. The first man we came to sat in the middle of the highway, blood gushing from a head wound to which he held a white cloth. We prayed for him, then moved on to another man whom we'd seen catapulted from one truck. He lay on his back, almost in the middle of the road. People already had gathered around his lifeless form. When the group found we were Christians, they backed up, allowing us room to pray. All vital signs were gone, but I was sure I was to command life to return to his body.

"Lord, put the spirit back into this man so he can live."

Instantly, he stirred and began to breathe. Excitement rippled through the crowd as we left to continue on to Jaggayyapet. When we saw a constable half an hour later, we reported the accident.

Upon arriving at the meeting site we found the advance party constructing the pendell. It would protect about eight thousand people from the hot sun. I would be amazed again at the incredible number of people who squeezed themselves into an area, sitting cross-legged, shoulder-to-shoulder.

Ten thousand handbills had been passed out and posters hung throughout the surrounding fifty villages. (As we traveled, we saw posters everywhere, many mutilated. Muslims and other factions, we supposed, were the culprits.)

Large crowds filled the pendell for every service. I was told that an elderly mother had instructed her four deaf and dumb married sons to attend the meetings. They ranged in age from twenty-eight to thirty-three and sat together in front of the dirt dias. While I spoke, every now and then they would point to their ears and open mouths.

The first few times they came for prayer I simply prayed for their healing. However, on the fourth night I rebuked the deaf and dumb spirit, commanding it to come out in the Name of Jesus. Still there was no evidence of healing.

"Why isn't God healing these men?" I was asked.

"Be patient," I replied.

On the last night of the meetings, while Philip supervised the dismantling of the pendell, one of the brothers touched him on the shoulder. Then he began voicing sounds for the first time since he'd been born. Philip, looking him in the eyes, spoke very slowly in English.

"Praise the Lord," he said.

"Praise the Lord," the man repeated.

The people who remained began rejoicing at the miracle God had performed.

A few minutes later, never having heard spoken words before, the young man spoke in his native tongue. "When will God heal my brothers so they can speak?" he asked.

Almost immediately his three brothers' ears and mouths were opened, too.

I learned that their father had chided his wife for sending their sons to the services, wondering what good it would do. It was foolish, he had said.

Word of this tremendous miracle spread quickly throughout the village, and people glorified God.

At this same meeting, a lady was carried in on a stretcher and placed to the far right of the dias. She was paralyzed. Since it was our custom to pray over every person, when we finished praying for others, each night her husband, Philip and I prayed for her.

The first night as we prayed she began to move. The next night when we went to her cot and prayed, she sat up. On the third night she not only sat up, but threw her legs over the side of the cot.

"Help me up," she commanded, and stood to her feet.

When we prayed on the fourth night, she repeated all of this and then took a few steps. We weren't at all surprised that on the fifth night she was able to walk home. (See testimonial letter #8.)

Typhoon warnings during these meetings forced us to pray against the predicted storm. We knew torrential rains and winds would destroy the pendell. Our faith was rewarded when the storm moved in a different direction, baffling the officials. Only a few raindrops fell. God had moved again in our behalf.

The first year, after I had arrived in India, God had given me a word that many healings would be complete after people returned home. Letters, especially this third year, confirmed that this was exactly the way God worked. I believe it kept the crowds from putting the emphasis on a man. Receiving the manifestation of their healings at home caused them to keep their eyes on Jesus.

We were thrilled to hear, too, that people threw away their idols once they met Jesus as Savior and Healer.

After checking through customs one year, Pastor Dwight Craver and I boarded a train for Ongol, where we'd hold the first series of meetings.

"Do you recognize that man across from us?" Dwight asked.

I didn't.

"He was the high-ranking policeman who watched while we came through customs." However, he'd exchanged the uniform for plain clothes.

"He's probably following us," I answered with a little concern. We'd need to be careful.

The man got off ahead of us when we arrived at our destination. Fortunately, there stood Philip.

"Inspector Philip, what case are you on?" the man quizzed. They knew each other from their days together in the police.

"I'm here to meet some Americans," Philip replied. "And you?"

"I'm here to follow some Americans."

Just then we exited the train for a warm and welcome reunion with Philip. The man quickly saw the connection, which established our credibility, and he left.

Had Philip not been there, however, we'd have been followed. Then if we'd spoken anything, especially about Jesus, which the police didn't like, we'd have been put out of India and never allowed to return.

We were thankful for the freedom we could enjoy, thanks to Pastor Philip.

\* \* \* \* \* \*

I peered through the darkness to see the thousands I'd been told had gathered for the meeting. But the lights surrounding the platform only illuminated the immediate area.

We were in Kazipet, one of three large cities in the region. I made a quick mental comparison of this stadium with the modern American ones. No colorful graduated seating filled this railroad-owned gathering place — only bare ground where Indian nationals would push together to hear their beloved Indira Ghandi, other government officials, or view a sporting event. A long, high cement wall surrounded the grounds and a steel-braced metal roof protected the tall cement dias where we stood. Now it would be a hallowed place.

Since we couldn't bill these as Christian services, our posters had advertised healing meetings. After the first night, thousands crowded into the arena, toting straw pads on which to sit.

When word reached the local rail manager that people wanted to accept Jesus, he canceled the remainder of our services. Hindus who had witnessed some of the many healings approached the man. They related miracles — God opening blind eyes, deaf ears, causing the lame to walk.

"Can your god do that?" they asked.

The question demanded consideration.

"You may have your meetings," the manager conceded, apologizing as fear replaced his forceful stubbornness.

A Catholic air force officer called one day, asking to see me. We were skeptical of such requests, knowing there were those desiring to kill us. I remembered the high-caste Hindu whose wife had become a Christian. She then invited us to their home for dinner. Philip, cautious, had sent Lilly to cook with the woman and watch the preparation of the meal, since poisonings were common. The food was fine and the whole family received Jesus.

But, still careful, Philip advised me to arrange to meet the officer at a conspicuous tourist spot. Soon he arrived with his aide.

"I came to you for prayer last night," he reported, "and felt a power I've never felt before." He had fallen under God's anointing. "It was a wonderful feeling, but what happened?"

I asked if he'd uttered any strange words. He hadn't. "The Holy Spirit touched you, but now you're to be baptized in the Holy Spirit." I put one hand on him and prayed quietly. Immediately he began praying in an unknown language. I watched as he left rejoicing in the new life he'd found in Jesus.

During the week we set out for the remote, primitive village of Killikunta, where we'd dedicate a cornerstone for a church building. Land had been donated for the project. The vice president of the village, I was told, hated Christianity and violently opposed the building of a church. But when I saw him sitting against a tree, I was led to call him forward. A disease plaguing his body quickly left as we prayed, and then he wanted to become a Christian. A broad smile spread across his brown face as he was set free.

In Kazipet we conducted morning teachings on the rooftop of a house. During one session, a young epileptic man had a seizure. We prayed, taking authority in Jesus' Name, and the young man was delivered.

When we arrived at the fourth meeting in Kazipet, a special sense of God's power filled the stadium. Right away I spied an attractive Indian woman, perhaps in her early thirties. She was weaving from side to side down one aisle, tossing pebbles on the heads of various onlookers and laughing crazily with each toss. Six or eight pastors, on reaching the woman, attempted to grab her. But she effortlessly threw off every one of them. I later learned she'd twisted the head off her first baby and thrown the body into a well. Her Muslim husband had despaired of there being any hope for his insane wife.

Philip and I glanced at each other questioningly, but had a mutual knowledge that it wasn't time to deal with her. As the service progressed, she became more active.

I stood to speak, Philip interpreting. By now the strange Muslim woman had made her way back through the crowd to the concrete stairs at the dias. As I stared into her eyes, a furtive fear replaced her devilish, mocking grin. It was time to act. Quickly I leapt down the stairs, running after the thin, fleeing form as she headed for the nearest gate. Reaching her, I touched the back of her head.

"In the Name of Jesus," I yelled. She spun around, bewilderment filling her dark eyes.

"Come out in the Name of Jesus," I then commanded,

touching her forehead. Over into the hot dust she fell, screaming. She stood, screamed, and fell again while I returned to the platform to finish my message. Every now and then I'd hear another scream. Seven times the scene was repeated until, finally, she arose, totally delivered. Now free, at the end of the service she received Jesus along with her grateful, weeping husband, ready to renounce his Muslim faith.

It reminded me of a service in Guntar my first year in India, when several people had been delivered in a crowd of about fifteen hundred. "In the Name of Jesus," I'd spoken, and two or three Hindus were picked off their feet, hurled by God's Spirit, and had landed in the dust ten to fifteen feet away. None of us had ever seen such a thing.

"What were the strange words I heard?" I asked Philip, referring to the Tellegu they'd shouted while being hurtled through the air.

" 'We'll leave. We can't stand the heat,' " Philip had replied. The Holy Spirit had indeed conquered the demonic forces.

This night in Kazipet I'd spoken of the Holy Spirit, starting in Genesis, moving to Joel and ending in Acts. "If you want this gift of the Holy Spirit, stand and come up front!" was the invitation I issued at the close. About three hundred ran forward.

"I'm to pray from here, Philip," I said, and prayed a general prayer in contrast to the usual prayer over each individual. I didn't know I was about to see one of the greatest outpourings of God's Spirit I'd ever witness in all of India.

I'd had the people lift their hands as I prayed. Suddenly, the air was charged with God's power. People began dancing and jumping before the Lord. New languages flowed from their mouths. Shouts of praise rang throughout the stadium. I thought of the thousands who received on the day of Pentecost as I gazed at these who appeared drunk in the Spirit.

An asthmatic woman fell under a mighty anointing. Her fourteen-year-old daughter attempted to pull her mother up, but upon contact she too fell over in the Spirit. The alcoholic husband, upon touching his wife, began dancing as if on a pogo stick, jumping and turning while praising God in another tongue. His wife began speaking words of knowledge in Tellegu. "Someone's being healed of cancer," she said, and a nearby woman was immediately released from the disease. When the mother and daughter were able to stand, all three witnessed to the miracles God had performed. The daughter lovingly embraced her "new" parents —her mother healed of asthma, her father delivered from alcoholism.

Now crowds began rushing in from the busy streets outside the stadium. They'd heard the commotion and came to find out what was happening. Over they fell in the Spirit, too, praying in new languages; but most importantly, receiving the Jesus we'd preached.

A businessman in Western dress looked on curiously nearly ten feet from me. Suddenly he was knocked over by the Spirit and landed in a row of bicycles. For half an hour he lay face down in the brown dirt.

We knew the danger of trying to make converts, but a new boldness sprang up within me.

"Anyone wanting to receive Jesus Christ, stand," I shouted to the crowd. When everyone stood, I thought perhaps they'd misunderstood my words. But as Philip led the thousands in a salvation prayer, I knew God had performed a miracle in the hearts of the seeking Indians. Because of these meetings, a pastor invited me to his large Baptist Church to speak.

"What are my limitations?" I asked.

"None," the pastor replied, and we enjoyed a beautiful service together. Many baptisms in the Spirit and healings resulted.

After Kazipet, our next meeting site was in the wilderness outside Katapalli. Six of us crowded into a tiny Fiat for the all-day trip. Some of our luggage and supplies we'd jammed into the trunk. The rest was tied onto the roof.

We headed toward the mountains. For several miles we traveled through a field which was less rutted than the nearby road. We dodged stubble and cacti. Still, it posed less problems than the several inches of dust on the narrow road. And it was smoother. How funny it seemed to see a bus or truck plying the field with us here and there.

Soon it was night and we were in Noxlite territory. (Noxlites are bands of criminals who specialize in ambushing travelers.) They'd been killing and robbing in this area just prior to our arrival.

Suddenly a thumping interrupted our travel: a flat tire. The danger of Noxlites and cobras filled the night's blackness. While some of the travelers worked on the tire, others of us banged on metal and sang, hoping the noise would ward off both dangers.

With no further misfortune we arrived at the forest tribal community, nearly three hours late. Colored streamers greeted us along with smiling villagers. Although scheduled for three nights of meetings, we could hold only one since there was no place for us to stay. Still, we saw God's hand at work with the same manifestations of His power as we'd seen in other villages. A sick Hindu priest, painted and in his priestly robes, came for prayer. After being healed he gave his life to Christ.

At two a.m. we arrived back at the facility where we were to sleep. With a government-issued order that we be out by five a.m., we were on the road again after a brief three hours' sleep.

A few hours later the car lurched to a stop. We climbed out to find the tie rod had dropped off, leaving the wheels aimed out in separate directions. One bolt was missing, the other hung loosely from its hold. With thin rope we pulled the ends in, lining up the wheels by "eye-ball engineering," and snugging up the one bolt.

We drove carefully for hours until finally we reached the next town. At a garage (a piece of canvas supported by four poles), we instructed the mechanics on the fixing of our little car, aiding them at the same time.

Tired, hot and dusty, nonetheless we rejoiced in all we'd seen God do. Neither India nor we would ever be the same again.

## Letter # 8

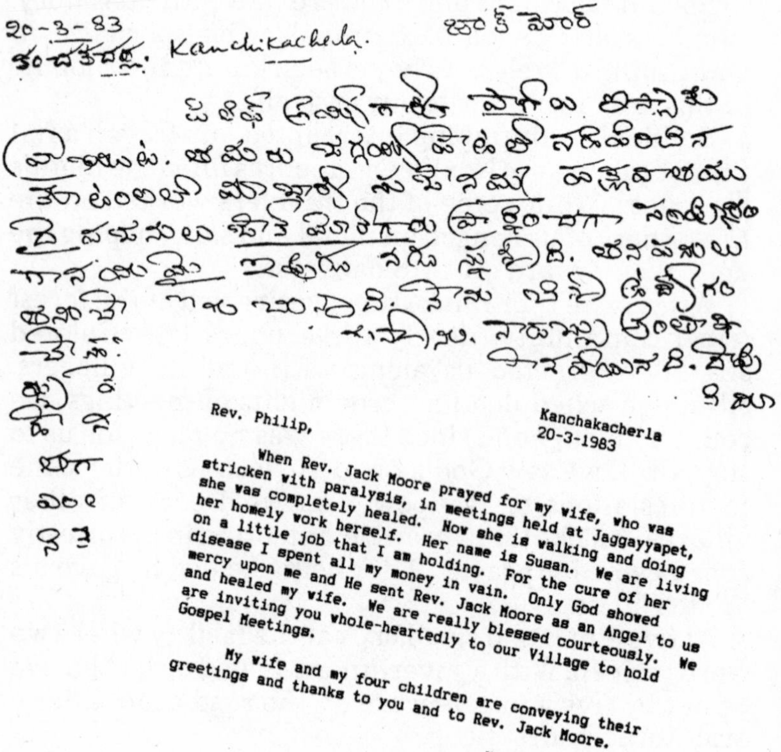

*[handwritten Telugu text]*

Rev. Philip,

Kanchakacherla
20-3-1983

When Rev. Jack Moore prayed for my wife, who was stricken with paralysis, in meetings held at Jaggayyapet, she was completely healed. Now she is walking and doing her homely work herself. Her name is Susan. We are living on a little job that I am holding. For the cure of her disease I spent all my money in vain. Only God showed mercy upon me and He sent Rev. Jack Moore as an Angel to us and healed my wife. We are really blessed courteously. We are inviting you whole-heartedly to our Village to hold Gospel Meetings.

My wife and my four children are conveying their greetings and thanks to you and to Rev. Jack Moore.

Yours obediently,

P. Esaach
Kanchakacherlee
Nandigama Tuluk
Krisna District

Below is a collage of only a few
of the Tellegu letters received from India.

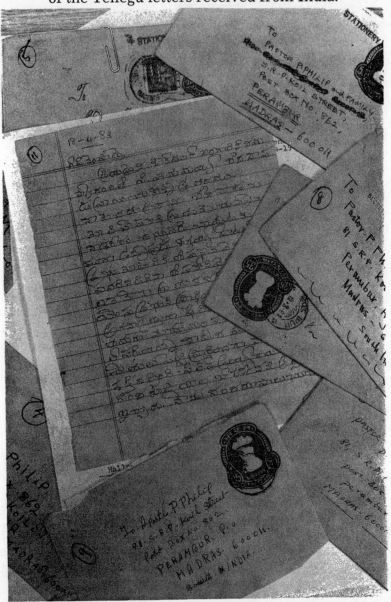

## Letter # 9

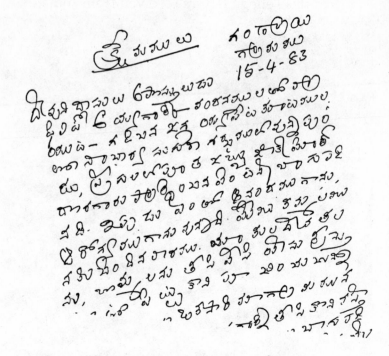

Gandrayi
15-4-1983

The Servant of God and Apostle Philip,

Writing with greetings to you. My wife Suguna was instantly healed of an ulcer in her uterus when she was prayed for by Rev. Jack Moore in the Jaggayyapet Meetings. She was also relieved of her intestinal trouble. Now she is completely healthy and happy. We are Hindus. We threw away the idols of various Goddesses from our house and we are praying to Jesus, hanging a photo of Jesus in our house. We will be very happy if you kindly bring Rev. Jack Moore to our village once. By that the Hindus in this village will get healed and keep aloof from worshiping the idols having confirmed their faith in Jesus, who is the real God. It is my earnest desire.

Convey our greetings to Sister.

Expecting your arrival.

Your Spiritual Son
Ganta Venkatesuarlu
Gandrdu Village
Jaggayyapet Taluk
Krishna District

## Letter # 3

25-4-83

*[handwritten letter in Telugu script]*

Mangolu Village
25-4-83

Rev. Philip,

I am conveying my thanks to you and writing in all humbleness. In the Jaggayyapet Meetings when the Angel of God, Jack Moore prayed for me I was immediately healed of my stomach cancer. I had the habit of eating earth balls and coal pieces. But it is now now. I have two daughters. I am a widow. Now, freed from my disease, I am able to work hard so that I may provide food to my daughters who are like destitutes. Now I am witnessing that Jesus is the Savior and there is no God except Jesus. I request you to pray for me and for my children. My hearty greetings to Sister and Elders there.

Yours obediently,
Kolla Achchamina
Mongollu Village
Jaggayyapet Teluk
Krishna District

## Letter # 11

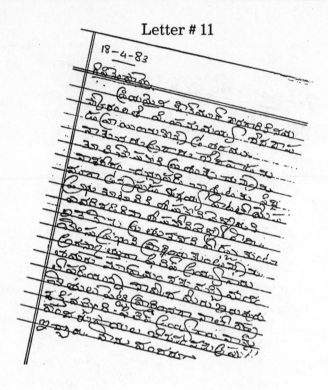

Gopinenipalem
18-4-1983

Beloved Jack Moore,

    My humble greetings to you and a humble letter to
you. I am illiterate and I am a poor man. I am living on
my earnings as a worker in the fields. I was paralyzed in
my body and was at the stage of death. When you held
meetings at Jaggayyapet, I wanted to attend the meetings
earnestly. Though I requested many people to take me to
the meetings, nobody came forward to help me. Thinking
that there was no hope for me to live, I began to weep and
pray to Jesus. But suddenly you and Pastor Philip came to
my Village, saw me bed-ridden, and you both prayed for me
laying your hands upon me. Immediately an unknown power
entered into me. And with great generosity Rev. Philip
gave one hundred Rupees to me for my feeding. A very long
time ago I saw a hundred Rupee note. After having a sound
sleep I woke up and I began to walk. Seeing this miracle
my wife, my children and the people of my Village felt
wondered. Hallelujah! Now I have a longing to see you once
again.

Yours obediently,
P. Hanumayya

# Chapter Thirty-two

# "I Could Kill You!"

*"...greater is he that is in you, than he that is in the world"* (I John 4:4).

I was on a return trip from India, stopping to minister in parts of Europe and Scandinavia on my way home. The streamlined Nord East Express carried me from Holland to Denmark. I settled late at night into the quiet and comfort of one of the compartments.

About one a.m. a group of youth, many carrying beer cans, boarded the train. Two of the young men entered my compartment, to my dismay. One lit a cigarette.

"The smoke bothers me," I told them, with a reminder that this was a non-smoking area. They politely stepped outside the enclosure.

I felt led to initiate conversation, asking them about themselves. They were Swedish and warmed to me when I spoke of my Swedish background.

"Are you Christians?" I asked.

One answered that he'd once been a Christian and his mother had recently been encouraging him to recommit his life to Jesus Christ. The other said he'd grown up knowing about God through his family, but had never acted on his knowledge.

He further spoke about always having a problem at the German border. He'd lost his passport and had no proper documentation. Once he was even put off the train.

I suggested we pray about it, which I did. At the border, the customs officer glanced at the paper the boy presented, okaying his passage.

"May I remind you we prayed?" I said afterward when the young man looked surprised.

Before I'd left Denmark, the people with whom I'd stayed had packed me a huge lunch of sandwiches and fruit, much more than I could eat. Now I saw the reason. I could share with two hungry boys, not only some spiritual food, but physical food as well.

It reminded me that while in Holland, I got a call from a seventeen-year-old boy who spoke perfect English. His mother, a Christian, had been praying for her son. She urged him to call me just for the opportunity of conversing in English, knowing I'd share Jesus with him. We met and chatted several times, became friends, and soon the boy received the Lord.

I was grateful for these times God gave me to share the Gospel as I traveled.

I spent a week in Denmark with a dear pastor, Karl, and his family, speaking at their church. Their home borders the building housing the "Mission Possible" ministry. I was given lovely accommodations on the top level of that building.

I enjoyed my fellowship in my friends' home and in their church. Now, however, I was to head for Sweden, just across the Baltic Sea, to visit another church.

Before I left, Karl asked me to pray that he'd find a buyer for his car. God answered our prayer, but it left him with no way to pick me up on my return. I'd have to find my way across the city. The directions were elaborate. First, I'd travel by airboat, then bus, and finally by train across Copenhagen before arriving back at their home.

When I finished with the ministry in Sweden, the man designated to take me to the boat never showed. I ran the eight or ten blocks from the church, toting all my luggage. Out of breath, I got to the dock just in time to learn that although I had a return ticket, I had no reservation for that day.

"I don't know if we can get you on," the ticket agent said, instructing me to stand to the side with others, also minus reservations. I watched while many people lined up for the boat and boarded.

"Lord, please save a seat for me," I asked, and was thankful to get the last one.

Upon disembarking, I hurried to the ticket counter for a bus ticket. Pornographic magazines lay in front of me. So shocked and repulsed was I at the blatant filth that I dropped my luggage and change. Coins rolled in every direction and I stooped to retrieve them. After gathering my belongings again, I got to the bus, only to find it wasn't the right one. I'd been given the wrong number. Finally I found my bus and listened carefully for the streets, trying to interpret the Danish.

Once at the rail station, I stepped down the stairs, asking people along the way if I was headed for the right train. On a bench parallel to the tracks sat a young boy, feet extended into the busy path of travelers. He held a pornographic magazine and was absorbed in its contents.

"You shouldn't be reading that!" I yelled, kicking the bottom of his feet as I spoke. My reaction surprised us both.

A drunk staggered up to me next, jabbering unintelligibly in my face. After asking him to repeat himself, he yelled, "You just don't want to understand!"

Finally finding my train, I sighed in relief. It was beautiful, offering pleasant comfort in its well-lighted, spacious cars. I chose a seat near the front in the non-smoking area, but facing the back. About sixteen people were scattered throughout the car, I noticed. A pretty girl sat opposite me.

Not aware that above my head was a listing of the stops, I asked her if this was the train I wanted, telling her where I was headed.

"Yes, it is, sir," she answered, to my delight, in excellent English.

Three seats back on my right, facing forward, was a large, surly-looking, unshaven man. He glared angrily at me.

"You have no business talking to that woman," he blurted out.

"I'm a Christian and have the freedom to talk to anyone," I replied. Upon my speaking the word "Christian," I saw the demonic possession in his red face. It was obvious, too, that he'd been drinking, his speech slurring as he spoke. Never had I seen such hatred.

"You're a dirty...." he shouted. "You can't do that!"

"I am a man of God and there's no harm in what I did."

Upon hearing God's Name, he was even more furious. Several more names, profanities and curses spewed from his mouth.

Most of the other passengers were women, I saw, as I glanced around looking for men who could come to my physical defense if necessary. Two well-dressed men, businessmen I presumed, whom I thought might be of help suddenly left when the man began his rantings.

Don't leave me now, I thought, and began praying out loud in tongues, while in my mind I asked God for protection.

"What are you doing?" the man yelled.

"God, please send a policeman or have him leave," I prayed. Suddenly, the irate man went out into the aisle, and with unsteady steps made his way past me. The automatic doors opened behind me and he entered the middle compartment. I hoped he was preparing to get off at the next stop, but quickly switched myself into the facing seat, not wanting the man at my back.

Just as quickly, he reentered the car and now loomed over me, evil filling his face.

"You know, I could kill you!" he screamed, wild eyes staring into mine. He flexed the muscles in his huge upraised arms, extending from his wrestler-like frame.

"Go ahead," I challenged in calm, measured words out of the peace I felt inside.

"Why aren't you scared?" he shouted.

"I am a man of God, and God protects me. You can't do anything to me."

With that, I saw fear replace the hatred and he began to back away through the doors.

Suddenly the train stopped. We were at the next station. As the door opened, plainclothes policemen grabbed the demon-possessed man, whisking him away. Behind them were the two men who had left the train earlier. They reentered and one sat down opposite me.

"Sir, I work for the railroad," he said. "I had the conductor call ahead for the police when we saw your dilemma."

"You're an answer to prayer," I told him, grateful for the intervention God had provided. "I'm a pastor and I prayed for God to send someone."

As the train pulled out, I realized I'd just missed my stop. Another passenger instructed me to go to the next one and wait by the second track. I'd not need a further ticket, I was told. I stood out beside the tracks, alone, feeling quite lost. But, just as I'd been assured, a train arrived in a few minutes.

Finally I found my way back to Karl's. Relief flooded me after such a harrowing, troublesome trip.

Now I had a new problem. All my luggage was locked and I couldn't find the key. And I'd been given the keys to every floor in the building next door. But I was missing those, too. They'd been with my change. When I dropped everything at the bus station, they must have been scattered under the counter or into a corner. Fortunately, Karl worked in metals. After a while, he'd fashioned a working key for my luggage. From men who lived in the building next door, I was able to secure keys to the levels.

When I finally got to my room that night, I dropped to my knees to thank God for His help and protection. I was grateful, too, that this day had ended.

# Chapter Thirty-three

# Twilight

*"Therefore I was left alone, and saw this great vision, and there remained no strength in me: for my comeliness was turned in me into corruption, and I retained no strength"* (Dan. 10:8).

I step into the empty sanctuary where the flock under my leadership gather. I take a seat, gaze at the pulpit and sense God's Presence as I'm wrapped in the quietness of this place He ordained.

Into my mind slips the memory of a time five months ago when I'd been plagued by hurt and disappointment because of church problems. I'd determined to fast and pray until receiving an answer and went on my face before God. Immediately I'd heard, "Stop looking at circumstances and people. Look to Me." I wondered how I could lose sight of such elementary truth.

I had walked out of my study just moments after entering. The days I'd been prepared to spend weren't required as I repented of my wrong focus.

Now as I sit in the stillness, I thank God for speaking to me, straightening my steps.

I review the highlights of the ministry with which He's entrusted me. I wonder how much time is left before Jesus' return. It's 1989. I've heard God speak. In a vision, He's shown me the shortness of time.

I recall a vision from the late seventies. I'd been praying, praising and singing as I drove, when suddenly two black parallel lines appeared. They seemed miles apart, just above the horizon in the morning sky. I immediately understood that the space between the columns represented all of time from Adam and Eve until the return of Christ. In the Spirit I saw Abraham against the left line. Near to the right were the apostles. Surprising to me was the closeness of the Book of Acts to the end. As if using a classroom pointer, the Lord directed my attention to the tiny space between Acts and now. "This is where you are," He said.

I sensed the loving Presence of Christ as Mediator as He spoke words of reassurance.

Then the voice of God thundered in my spirit. At that moment, time seemed to stop. "This age as you know it is coming to an end," I heard. As the words reverberated, all breath seemed to be drawn from my lungs and I gasped for new air. Gripping the wheel, I pulled to the side of the highway. God's awesomeness, the gravity of His words, and the power of His voice and Presence were overwhelming, and I sat quietly for several moments. Then I remembered Daniel's words from Daniel 10:17. "For how can the servant of this my lord talk with this my lord? for as for me, straightway there remained no strength in me, neither is there breath left in me."

Finally able to speak, I prayed, "God, please, if You ever come this close to me again, give me a witness."

A few days later, while in a restaurant with two friends, the Lord interrupted our conversation. I saw one's living room. "Go there immediately to pray," He instructed. I shared His direction, and we obeyed. I was led to remove my shoes. Then I knelt and raised my hands in worship. Immediately I was out in the Spirit.

"I have provided you with two witnesses," the Lord

spoke through my own mouth. My friends sensed the special anointing on this time and began to record what they saw and heard. For three hours I communed in the spirit, unaware of time or surroundings. I was lifted into a dimension beyond my understanding.

At one point Jesus stood in front of me. His love flowed through me and I reached out, attempting to touch His feet. The intimacy defied description.

Then God presented Himself. His majesty, power and purity were so awesome that I tried to hide.

Suddenly I saw the cross beneath me. Although there was no pain, I felt a touch of Jesus' agony —agony so horrible it can't be compared with any earthly suffering. I felt my body being stretched taut.

"Oh Jesus ... You did it for me," I cried out. "You loved us ... You forgave us ... Oh, Jesus." And I wept. Never before had I felt such a depth in God's love as expressed in the sacrifice of His Son. I could never doubt His love after that day.

The lengthening shadows remind me it's time to go home. I think of the coming spiritual night Jesus speaks of in John 9, "... when no man can work." As I head out into the twilight, I know I must continue to obey; I must continue to serve.

# Afterword

I've shared many experiences, unique by worldly standards, but spiritually the norm for those whose total faith is in God's Word. To those seeking, I'd advise: Don't seek an experience; seek Jesus. Seek to know Him as Savior and Lord, for establishing a relationship with Him is the starting point. Seek to know Him as Baptizer in the Holy Spirit; seek to know Him as Healer.

We must be bold, grounded in the Word of God, and in daily communion with Him in prayer, for it is out of this Life-flow that we receive Life. Fruit of the Spirit (Galatians 5) is the natural product of this Life.

We must never be ashamed of the Gospel, regardless of who we're with or where we are. We're not to flaunt our faith, but walk lovingly and in humility. Finally, we must fellowship in a church where Jesus is proclaimed and extend our love to help the poor.

The gifts of the Spirit are manifested in my various experiences. There are three gifts of revelation: wisdom, knowledge and discerning of spirits; three gifts of power: healings, miracles and faith; and three gifts of utterance: prophecy, tongues and interpretation of tongues. Again, I caution that one not seek a gift, but the Giver. His Word says, in First Corinthians 12, that He, the Holy Spirit, uses the gifts through us as He chooses, to build us, His Church.

I admonish those in the Body to walk in integrity —as if Jesus were there in the flesh. Be overcomers; be strong. He's coming soon. We must be ready.